The Lincoln–Douglas debates of 1858

ABRAHAM LINCOLN

1858

TABLE OF CONTENTS

PREFACE

THIS VOLUME which comprises the memorable debates between Mr. Lincoln and Judge Douglas during the Senatorial campaign of 1858, is presented to the members and guests at the banquet given by the Association on the One Hundred and Second Anniversary of Mr. Lincoln's birth.
The Lincoln Centennial Association.

FORMER GUESTS OF HONOR

The Right Honorable James Bryce, The British Ambassador. The Honorable J. J. Jusserand, The French Ambassador.

The Honorable Jonathan P. Dolliver of Iowa.

The Honorable William Jennings Bryan of Nebraska. The Honorable Robert T. Lincoln of Illinois. The Honorable N. C. Blanchard of Louisiana. The Honorable Fred. T. Dubois of Idaho. The Honorable Charles S. Deneen of Illinois. The Honorable John W. Noble of Missouri. The Honorable Richard Yates of Illinois. The Honorable Peter S. Grosscup of Illinois. The Honorable William H. Seaman of Wisconsin. The Honorable Albert B. Anderson of Indiana.

The Honorable Alfred Orendorff of Illinois.

The Honorable James S. Harlan of Washington, D. C. The Honorable William A. Rodenburg of Illinois. The Honorable John P. Hand of Illinois. Dr. Booker T. Washington of Alabama.

The Honorable Howland J. Hamlin of Illinois.

The Honorable William H. Stead of Illinois. The Honorable Francis G. Blair of Illinois. Deceased.

INCORPORATORS

Hon. Melville W. Fuller, Chief Justice U. S. Supreme Court.

Hon. Shelby M. Cullom, United States Senator. Hon. Albert J. Hopkins. Hon. Joseph G. Cannon, Member of Congress. Hon. Adlai E. Stevenson. Hon. Charles S. Deneen, Governor of Illinois. Hon. John P. Hand, Justice Supreme Court Illinois. Hon. J Otis Humphrey, Judge U. S. District Court. Hon. James A. Rose, Secretary of State. Hon. Ben F. Caldwell. Hon. Richard Yates. Melville E. Stone, Esq., New York. Horace White, Esq., New York. John W. Bunn, Esq. Dr. William Jayne. OFFICERS. President.... J Otis Humphrey Vice-President... John W. Bunn Secretary.... Philip B. Warren Treasurer.. . J- H. Holbrook DIRECTORS. Shelby M. Cullom, J Otis Humphrey, John W. Bunn, Charles S. Deneen, James A. Rose, Deceased. The Lincoln Centennial Association

EXECUTIVE COMMITTEE.
John W. Bunn, Thomas Rees, Victor Bender, George Reisch, CHnton L. Conlding, James A. Rose, Shelby M. Ciillom, Nicholas Roberts, Charles S. Deneen, Edgar S. Scott, E. A. Hall, George B. Stadden, Logan Hay, Louis C. Taylor, J Otis Humphrey, Jas. R. B. VanCleave, William Jayne, Philip B. Warren, William B. Jess, Howard K. Weber, Edward D. Keys, Bluford Wilson, George Pasfield, Jr W. F. Workman, Edward W. Payne, Loren E. Wheeler.

MEMBERSHIP COMMITTEE.
Nicholas Roberts, Verne Ray, James A. Easley, Latham T. Souther, Arthur D. Mackie.

PUBLICITY COMMITTEE.
James A. Rose, Henry Merriam, Jas. R. B. VanCleave, Thomas Rees.

BANQUET COMMITTEE.
George B. Stadden, John McCreery, Philip Barton Warren, Walter McClellan Allen.

MUSIC COMMITTEE.
Robert C. Brown, Albert Guest, Clark B. Shipp.

SPEAKER'S COMMITTEE.
Shelby M. Cullom, Charles S. Deneen, J Otis Humphrey.

SOUVENIR AND PRINTING COMMITTEE.
Jas. R. B. VanCleave, Archibald L. Bowen, Harrison C. Blankemeyer.

CEREMONIES COMMITTEE.
James A. Rose, Francis G. Blair, J. H. Collins,

DECORATION COMMITTEE.
Henry Abels, H. D. Swirlcs, George B. Helmle,, Frank S. Dickson.

LIFE MEMBERS.
ARKANSAS, LUXORA, S. E. Simonson. CALIFORNIA, San Francisco, Geo. N. Armsby. COLORADO, Colorado Springs, Jos. W. Norvell. DISTRICT OF COLUMBIA. Washington. Shelby M. CuUom, Melville W. Fuller,
Geo. C. Rankin, Wm. Barrett Ridgely. INDIANA, WiNIMAC, Moses A. Dilts. IOWA, OSKALOOSA, J. F. McNiel, MASSACHUSETTS, Amherst, E. F. Leonard. MINNESOTA, St. Paul. Asa G. Briggs. MISSOURI, St. Louis, Wells H. Blodgett, W. L. Desnoyers, V. E. Desnoyers, David R. Francis, Warrick M. Hough, Ridgely Hudson, B. C. Winston. NEW YORK, New York City, John W. Aymar, Horace White, Melville E. Stone. OHIO, Lima, B. R. Stephens. OKLAHOMA, ViNITA, Joseph A. Gill, PENNSYLVANIA, Philadelphia, William H. Lambert. WISCONSIN, Milwaukee, H. T. Whitcomb. ILLINOIS. Aurora, Albert J. Hopkins. Ashland, Edwin C. Beggs. Auburn, W. W. Lowry. Belleville. Wm. U. Halbert. Bethany, John A. Freeland, A. R. Scott. Bloomington, J. H. Cheney, Lafayette Funk, Frank Gillespie, Thos. C. Kerrick, John T. Lillard, Adlai E. Stevenson. Buffalo Hart, John S. Hurt. Buffalo, Henry C. Garvey, Oliver McDaniel. Cairo, F. A. DeRosset, Geo. Parsons. Cambridge, John P. Hand. Carlinyille, John I. Rinaker, Robert B. Shirley. Carthage, James

Gibson. Deceased. Carbondale,

Geo. W. Smith.

Chicago, Jacob M. Appel, J.'Ogden Armour, A. C. Bartlett, Wm. S. Beale, W. L. Brown, William T. Church, Alex Chystraus, C. E. Crafts, Richmond Dean, Chas. S. Deneen, Theodore Finn, Peter S. Grosscup, Ernest A. Hamill, J. T. Harahan, Geo. B. Harris, Jesse Holdom, Frank H. Jones, Nicholas R. Jones, Robt. T. Lineohi, Willard M. McEwen, Wm. H. MiteheU, Edward Morris, Edward H. Morris, James H. Roberts, W. C. Seipp, Frank C. Shepherd, Byron L. Smith, Orson Smith, A. A. Sprague, W. H. Swett, Elijah N. Zoline, Champaign, Euclid B. Rogers. Charleston, Frank K. Dunn Chatham, Ben. F. Caldwell, Danville, Walter J. Grant, Wm. R. Jewell, Frank Lindley, John L. Watts, Joseph G. Cannon, Decatur, Everett J. Brown, Hugh Crea, O. B. Gorin, Milton Johnson, E. S. McDonald, Joseph J. Sheehan. Divernon, Charles G. Brown. Dixon,

S. H. Bethea.

Donovan, John Nelson. Elkhart, John D. G. Oglesby. East St. Louis, J. B. Maguire. EVANSTON, J. Seymour Currey. Fakmersville, John Ball. Galesburg, W. E. Terry. Granite City, R. E. Neidringhaus. Hamilton, Edmund P. Denton. Harrisburg, I. R. Tuttle. Jacksonville, Thos. B. Orear, Miller Weir, H. B. Carriel. Andrew Russel. Joliet, W. W. Smith. Kankakee, Len Small. Lanesville P. J. Kent, La Salle, F. W. Matthiessen, Litchfield, J. Carl Dodds, Lincoln, J. A. Lucas.

Deoeaed. Madison,

F. A. Garesehe. Mattoon, Jas. W. Craig. Mechanicsburg, W. S. Bullard. Morrison, F. E. Ramsey. Mt. Sterling, J. F. Regan. Mt. Vernon, W. C. Arthurs. New Berlin, B. W. Brown, J. Brown Hitt. Newman, Scott Burgett. W. M. Young. Oregon, Frank O. Lowden, Ottawa, M. T. Moloney. Pawnee. Edward Baxter, Thos. A. Shepherd, Frank Morrell. Paxton, Charles Bogardus. Pearl City, Charles Musser. Peoria, Edward W. Henry, H. W. Lynch, Robert H. Lovett, I. C. Pinknev, P. G. Renniek, Joseph A. Veil, Henry Abels, 5 Alfred Adams, O. G. Addleman, Walter McC. Allen,

Jas. H. Anderson,

Oscar Ansell, W. P. Armstrong, O. B. Babcock, L. L. Bacchus, Chas. F. Bauman, Deceased. Springfield. Raymond V. Bahr, H. S. Beckemeyer, Victor E. Bender, Richard Ball, John A. Barber, H. E. Barker, S. A. Barker,

James H. Barkley, A. J. Barnes, Edgar S. Barnes, Pittspield, Harry Higbee. PONTIAC, J. M. Lyon. QUINCY, Edward J. Parker, W. S. Warfield, Fred Wilms. RrVERTON, John Deal. Rochester, Ira F. Twist, ROCKPORD, Wm. W. Bennett, Robert Rew. RUSHVILLE, John S. Little. Sharpsburg, O. S. Nash. Shelbyville, J. W. Yantis. Urbana, Edmund J. James. V AND ALIA, W. M. Farmer. Virginia,

Riehard W. Mills.

Virden, J. H. Shriver, Howard T. Wilson, Joseph N. Ross, WiLLIAMSVILLE, J. F. Prather, John W. Prather. W. B. Barry, Geo. A. Bates, Geo. H. Becker, Robert L. Berry, Chas. T. Biseh, Harold P. Bisch, John W. Black, Ira B. Blackstock, Francis G. Blair, HarrisonC. Blankemeyer, Frank H. Bode, Alfred Booth, C. M. Bowcoek, Archibald L. Bowen. Wm. A. Bradford, Jas. L. Brainerd, Charles Bressmer, John Bressmer, John E. Bretz, John F. Bretz, Geo. M. Brinkerhoff, Sr. Geo. M. Brinkerhoff, Jr. John H. Brinkerhoff, Stuart Broadwell, Milton Hay Brown, Owsley Brown, Robert C. Brown, Stuart Brown, W. H. Bruce, Fred Buck, Wm. A. M. Bunker, Geo. W. Bunn, Henrj' Bunn, Jacob, Bunn, John W. Bunn, Joseph F. Bunn, Yillard Bunn, Edmund Burke, Saml. T. Burnett, Wm. G. Burns, William J. Butler, J. F. Cadwallader, E. E. Cantrall, C. C. Carroll, Stanley Castle, E. L. Chapin, Geo. W. Chatterton, Sr. Henry L. Child, George E. Coe, Louis J. Coe, Harry E. Coe, Nathan Cole, L. H. Coleman, Logan Coleman, Louis G. Coleman, J. H. Collins, Clinton L. Conkling, Wm. H. Conkling, Geo. S. Connelly, James A. Connolly, A. E. Converse, A. L. Converse, Deceased. Henry A. Converse, Wm. O. Converse, Thomas Condell, T. J. Condon, W. H. Conway, Jas. L. Cook, John C. Cook, James A. Creighton,

A. N. J. Crook,

Shelby M. Cullom, L. A. Danner, Gaylord Davidson, Henry Davis, J. McCan Davis, Geo. Edward Day, Don Deal, Charles S. Deneen, V. E. Desnoyers, W. L. Desnoyers, D. A. DeVares, Isaac R. Diller, J. W. Diller, Henry A. Dirksen, Fred C. Dodds, R. N. Dodds, Thos. M. Dolan, Harry F. Dorwin, Shelby C. Dorwin, James E. Dowling, B. F. Drennan, Lincoln Dubois, Geo. C. Dunlop, E. J. Dunn, James A. Easley, R. H. Easley, A. W. Edward, Albert S. Edwards, Richard Egan, Anton Elshoff, Joseph Farris, Clarence W. Feaster, WiUiam Fetzer, Ed. J. Flynn, Frank R. Fisher, C. A. Fiske, Arthur M. Fitzgerald, J. G. Fogarty, John L. Fortado, John J. Foster, Carl D. Franlandlt;e, John B. Franz, C. A. Frazee, D. C. Frederick, James Furlong, M. B. Garber, G. J. George, Cornelius J. Giblin, George B. Gillespie, Frank Godley, Hugh J. Graham, James M. Graham, R. A. Guest,

Rudolph Haas, A. Lee Hagler, Elmer E. Hagler, Nathan Haider man, E. A. Hall, James A. Hall, Wathen Hamilton, Saml. J. Hanes, Wm. B. Hankins,

Edw. F. Hartman,

Frank L. Hatch, Pascal E. Hatch, Robt. E. Hatcher, Charles E. Hay, Logan Hay, E. F. Hazell, Ernest H. Helmle, George B. Helmle, J. C. Helper, G. B. Hemenway, J. E. Hemmiek, R. F. Herndon, Rev. Timothy Hickey, George C. Hickox, Howard T. Hicks, B. R. Hieronymus, Alonzo Hoff, J. H. Holbrook, W. M. Howard, James L. Hudson, Ridgely Hudson, Arthur F. Hughes, J Otis Humphrey, Otis S. Humphrey, R. G. Hunn, Charles H. Hurst, Harry L. Ide, Roy Ide, Edwin F. Irwin, Horace C. Irwin, A. C. James, Frank R. Jamison, William Jayne, James W. Jefferson, Roy T. Jefferson, Wm. B. Jess, Edward S. Johnson, James A. Jones, James T. Jones, M. A. Jones, Strother T. Jones, Charles P. Kane, Alvin S. Keys, Edward D. Keys, Edward L. Keys, George E. Keys, John M. Kimble, Richard F. Kinsella, Ben M. Kirlin, Carl Klaholt, Benjamin Knudson, Geo. N. Kreider, B. A. Lange, Geo. C. Latham Henry C. Latham, F. M. Legg, Jerome A. Leland, Warren E. Lewis, Gersham J. Little, G. L. Lloyd, John H. Lloyd, Rev. T. D. Logan, E. F. Lomelino, Fred W. Long, Harry T. Loper, John S. Lord, Henry B. Lubbe, T. B. Luby, John Lutz, Thos. E. Lyon, Arthur D. Maekie, Alex. B. Macpherson, J. F. Macpherson, John Maldaner, James M. Margrave, William Marlowe, John D. Marney, H. W. Masters, Robert Matheny, James H. Matheny, A. F. Maurer, O. F. Maxon, R. H. McAnulty, John McCreery, Deceased. James S. McCuUough, Frank M. McGowan, Harry 0. McGrue, J. F. McLennan, Henry B. McVeigh, John E. Melick, H. M. Merriam, J. F. Miller, L. S. Miller, Charles F. Mills, Lewis H. Miner, W. H. Minton, John P. Mockler, C. F. Mortimer, S. E. Munson, P. F. Murphy, Geo. W. Murray, Thos. J. Murray, Albert Myers, Lewis M. Myers, Harry W. Nickey, W. A. Northcott,

Alfred Orendorff,

James R. Orr, E. W. Osborne, James H. Paddock, H. C. Page, Geo. Thomas Palmer, George Pasfield, Sr., George Pasfield, Jr., Warren E. Partridge, Charles L. Patton, James W. Patton, William L. Patton, Wm. A. Pavey, Edward W. Payne, Jesse K. Pay ton, D. Lyman Phillips, Herman Fieri k, John C. Pierik, A. C. Piersel, John Pope, Fred W. Potter, Rufus M. Potts, Charles A. Power, H. T. Pride, Arthur E. Prince,

John A. Prince,

Edgar C. Pruitt, Henry G. Pyle, G. W. Quackenbush, John Quinlan, John P.

Ramsey, Albert H. Rankin, Isaac N. Ransom, Verne Ray, Horace S. Rearden, Roy R. Reece, Thomas Rees, Frank Reisch, George Reisch, Leonard Reisch, Henry C. Remann, Benjamin Rich, William Ridgley, Chas. D. Roberts, Nicholas Roberts, Chas. H. Robinson, Edward S. Robinson, Roy F. Rogers, John D. Roper, James A. Rose, C. H. Rottger, Albert Salzenstein, Emanuel Salzenstein, L. J. Samuels, M. D. Schaff, C. H. Schonbacher, F. L. Sehlierbach, Emil G. Schmidt, John S. Schnepp J. B. Seholes, Saml. D. Seholes, Charles Schuck, J. H. Schuck, Edgar S. Scott, John W. Scott, O. G. Scott,

Thomas W. Scott,

Roy M. Seeley, Richings J. Shand, William Sheehan, Lawrence Y. Sherman,

Chas. M. Shepherd,

Wm. B. Shepherd, Clark B. Shipp, John H. Sikes, A. W. Sikking, Frank Simmons, Geo. M. Skelly, Dewit W. Smith, E. S. Smith, Hal M. Smith, Wm. W. Smith, E. A. Snively, H. M. Solenberger, W. C. Sommer, Latham T. Souther, J. W. Southwiek, W. J. Spaulding, E. A. Stadden, Geo. B. Stadden, W. C. Starck, Wm. H. Stead, Geo. F. Stericker,

Heiiry A. Stevens,

J. H. Storj'. Sam'l J. Stout, R. H. Strongman, J. W. Stuart, Thos. W. Sudduth, Wm. H. SuUivan, W. W. Swett, Jr., H. G. Swirles, Louis C. Taylor, Deceasad. Will Taylor. E. R. Thayer, W. A. Townsend, H. H. Tuttle, Joseph W. Vance, Burke Vaneil, Jas. R. B. Van Cleave, Walter S. Van Duyn, Peter Vredenburgh, Sr., Robert O. Vredenburg, Thos. D. Vredenburg, Wm. R. Vredenburg, C. H. Walters, J. C. Walters, Philip B. Warren, Howard K. Weber, Charles Werner, Loren E. Wheeler, J. E. White, Henry C. Whittemore, Frank Weidlocher, Horace L. Wiggins, Lewis N. Wiggins, Harry T. Willett, Samuel J. Willett, Daniel T. WilUams, Bluford Wilson, G. M. Wilson, H. Clay Wilson, Henry W. Wilson, J. F. Wilson, Thomas W. Wilson, Chas. G. Wineteer, T. E. Wing, C. M. Woods, W. F. Workman, Richard Yates, John York, W. A. Young, William Zapf, Joseph Zimmerman, Chas. W. Zumbrook, Abbtttnnal 2jtff MtmbtYB. ILLINOIS. A. A. Anderson, Springfield. William H. Behrens, Carlinville. Frank L. Burton, Carlinville. A. Campbell Brown, Springfield. Charles T. Bauman, Springfield. Samuel A. Bullard, Springfield. Noah M. Cass, Springfield. J. A. Cousley, Alton. Ira C. Cople5^ Aurora. Prank S. Dickson, Springfield. J, Carl Dodds, Litchfield. D. Frank Fawcett, Springfield. David Felmley. Normal. J. H. Feltham, Springfield. A. P. Grout, Winchester. A. L.

Hereford, Springfield. Adelbert P. Higley, Springfield. Charles P. Hitch, Paris. W. J. Horn, Springfield. J. H. Hubbs, Prentice. S. H. Humphrey, Virden. W. M. Jageman, Springfield. A. J. Kennedy, Dekalb. Frank T. Kuhl, Springfield. Joseph Leiter, Chicago. Rodman C. O. Matheny, Springfield. R. N. McCauley, Normal. W. G. McRoberts, Peoria. A. H. McTaggert, Pana. Frank W. Morse, Chicago. W. H. Nelms, Springfield. Frank P. Norbury, Kankakee. J. B. Oakleaf, Moline. U. G. Orendorff, Canton. W. A. Orr, Springfield. P. J. O'Reilly, Springfield. William H. Parlin, Canton. A. J. Portch, Springfield. Carl M. Reisch, Springfield. Edward Reisch, Springfield. George Reisch, Jr., Springfield. Joseph Reisch, Springfield. W. E. Robinson, Springfield. C. W. H. Schuck, Springfield. Frank L. Shepherd, Chicago. Frank L. Smith, Dwight. George W. Smith, Carbondale. Albert D. Stevens, Springfield. J. Mack Tanner, Springfield. James W. Templeman, Springfield. Wm. E. Trautnian, East St. Louis. F. C. Wallbaum, Ashland. Joseph A. Weil, Peoria. Charles R. Wescott, Springfield. Frank D. Whipp, Springfield. Thomas Worthington, Jacksonville. MICHIGAN. Charles W. Post, Battle Creek. WISCONSIN. John E. Burton, Milwaukee. ABRAHAM LINCOLN. From a photograph In the collection of the Illinois Historical Library. Evidence seems to show that the negative was made at Charleston, Illinois, during the Campaign of 1858. The LLNCOtN Series, Vol. I COLLECTIONS OF THE ILLINOIS STATE HISTORICAL LIBRARY VOLUME III LINCOLN SERIES, VOL. I THE LINCOLN-DOUGLAS DEBATES OF 1858 EDITED WITH INTRODUCTION AND NOTES BY EDWIN ERLE SPARKS, PH. D. PRESIDENT OF THE PENNSYLVANIA STATE COLLEGE: SOMETIME PROFESSOR OF AMERICAN HISTORY IN THE UNIVERSITY OF CHICAGO Published by the Trustees of the ILLINOIS STATE HISTORICAL LIBRARY SPRINGFIELD, ILLINOIS

PREFACE

A new edition of the speeches made by Stephen A. Douglas and Abraham Lincoln in the set debate during the Illinois senatorial canvass of 1858 would seem a worthy and appropriate part of the general commemoration of the fiftieth anniversary of that event. While the campaign was local in its inception, it became national in its significance and in its results. The issues as brought out in the debate, especially in the speech of Douglas at Freeport, widened, if they did not open, the breach between him and the southern Democrats, made a split in the convention of 1860 a foregone conclusion, and thereby paved the way for Republican success and the election of Abraham Lincoln to the presidency. The debate also marked the high-tide of the "stump" method of campaigning; it furnishes, through the unusual space given to it in newspaper reports, an opportunity to study this unique phenomenon of frontier life; while the increasing number of printing presses, the extension of the mail routes, and consequent change in campaign methods, lend to this canvass the melancholy interest of a passing show. The speeches themselves are of a high order of debate, and of unusual import; those of Douglas set forth his untenable position and his impossible theory in the clearest terms; those of Lincoln state the arguments of the new Republican party as they had not been outlined before ; and the combined effect of the whole is a survey of the political aspect of the day not to be found elsewhere.

Many editions of the debates have been printed, beginning with that of 1860; a few have included speeches made by each participant, both before and after the set debates; some have added explanatory footnotes; but none have attempted to reproduce the local color from the press of the day. In this edition an effort is made by newspaper extracts and by reminiscences to give a picture of the crude though virile setting in this contest of two men so evenly matched in polemical power, yet so unlike in temperament and in physical appearance. Only those speeches are here reprinted which were delivered at the seven set meetings constituting in reality the Great Debate. The gist of the prior speeches is woven into the introduction.

The Columbus, Ohio, edition of 1860 is followed in this text, but the speeches as there reprinted have been compared with the originalsthose of Lincoln with the files of the Chicago Press and Tribune, and those of Douglas with the Chicago Timesand the changes which the Columbus edition made in the official reports are here shown in the footnotes; and there has been also incorporated in the text the numerous interruptions of the speeches by the audiences. In the present edition, the largest type indicates the editor's explanatory comments; the next largest shows quotations, the source being indicated at the head; and the smallest size of type denotes quoted matter within a quotation.

The descriptions and comments reprinted from the newspapers of the day are by no means exhaustive; fully one-half the matter originally collected was rejected for lack of space; but much of it was immaterial, being made up of denunciation and attempts to belittle the other side, predictions of victory, and general comment, which threw no light on the events of the debate. The amount of reminiscential matter was reduced by the same test. Such illustrations were selected as lent themselves to illuminating the subject-matter. In collecting the extracts and the illustrations, the editor has visited many places, has searched through scores of newspaper files, and has levied upon the courtesy of librarians and friends, to mention whose names would involve a list of impossible proportions. That the edition may be of service to the student as well as to the general reader; that it may aid in bringing to their true proportions these two great citizens of Illinois; and that it may reflect some credit upon the General Assembly of Illinois through whose beneficence it is made possible, is the hope that sustains a labor of love.

Edwin Erle Sparks
The University of Chicago
March 11, 1908

LINCOLN AND DOUGLAS

CHAPTER I. STUMP SPEAKING

The pioneers, who migrated with their families during the first half of the nineteenth century from the Atlantic Coast Plain to the Mississippi Valley found themselves cut off from the conveniences of life to which they had been accustomed, and cast into a compelling environment, where makeshifts and substitutes must answer for well-known utilities and contrivances. This was noticeable even in political campaigns. Lacking printing presses to disseminate party doctrines and public halls of sufficient size to accommodate the crowds at a party rally, the people of the frontier were wont to gather in some public square or in a grove of trees, where a temporary stand, or perhaps in very early days, the stump of a felled tree, answered the purpose of a rostrum from which the issues of the day were discussed by "stump" speakers. In the same way, the lack of churches on the frontier caused the substitution of groves as a place for holding "camp-meetings." Through campaign after campaign, both national and state, "stump" speaking continued until improved facilities for making longer journeys began to remedy western isolation and to remove western provincialism. At the same time, the increasing political activity of the printing press and the demands of modern business life gradually turned the people away from these picturesque gatherings of earlier times. Beginning with the campaign of 1824, in which a favorite son of Kentucky and a war-hero of Tennessee were championed in song and speech by their supporters in the Middle West, the political "stump" became the favorite hustings. The news that a leader was to "take the stump" in a certain district was sufficient promise of enlightenment on the political issues of the day in a region where newspapers and campaign literature were meager; and also the occasion was likely to afford a diversion in the way of rival processions and to furnish an opportunity of meeting one's friends and neighbors. The community which was favored as the scene of a political debate immediately awoke to unwonted activity. Banners were painted, flags flung from staff and building, and lithographs of rival candidates displayed in windows. Great barges or wagons, especially decorated for the occasion, were filled with "first voters," or with young women dressed to symbolize the political aspects of the campaign. Local merchants hurriedly stocked up on novelties likely to be in demand, while itinerant venders altered their schedules and hurried to the promising center of trade. Upon the public square each party erected a "pole" with a banner bearing the name of its candidates flying from the lofty top. The rural male voter did not appropriate to himself all the joys of the occasion, but the entire family "went to town," to enjoy the unusual day of diversion in the round of a monotonous and isolated life. A reporter connected with a New York newspaper was sent to Illinois to write up one of these "stump" campaigns, and both vividly and appreciatively he described the gathering of the people for the chief event of the summer:

"It is astonishing how deep an interest in politics this people take. Over long weary miles of hot and dusty prairie the processions of eager partisans come on foot, on horseback, in wagons drawn by horses or mules; men, women, and children, old and young; the half sick, just out of the last 'shake;' children in arms, infants at the maternal fount, pushing on in clouds of dust and beneath the blazing sun; settling down at the town where the meeting is, with hardly a chance for sitting, and even less opportunity for eating, waiting in anxious groups for hours at the places of speaking, talking, discussing, litigious, vociferous, while the war artillery, the music of the bands, the waving of banners, the huzzahs of the crowds, as delegation after delegation appears; the cry of the peddlers vending all sorts of ware, from an infalliable cure of 'agur' to a monster watermelon in slices to suit purchaserscombine to render the occasion one scene of confusion and commotion. The hour of one arrives and a perfect rush is made for the grounds; a column of dust is rising to the heavens and fairly deluging those who are hurrying on through it. Then the speakers come with flags, and banners, and music, surrounded by cheering partisans. Their arrival at the ground and immediate approach to the stand is the signal for shouts that rend the heavens. They are introduced to the audience amidst prolonged and enthusiastic cheers; they are interrupted by frequent applause; and they sit down finally amid the same uproarious demonstration. The audience sit or stand patiently throughout, and, as the last word is spoken, make a break for their homes, first hunting up lost members of their families, getting their scattered wagonloads together, and, as the daylight fades away, entering again upon the broad prairies and slowly picking their way back to the place of beginning." Special correspondence from Charleston, Illinois, to the New York Post, September 24, 1858.

The patience of the crowd in listening to lengthy speeches, as noted by this correspondent, finds many illustrations elsewhere. Three hours was the usual time allotted to a speaker. Sometimes after listening to a discussion of this length during the afternoon, the crowd would disperse for supper and then return to hear another speaker for an equal length of time during the evening. The spirit of fairness to both sides prompted the people to furnish one speaker with as large an audience as the other enjoyed. This spirit was manifested at Peoria in 1854 as the following extract from a contemporary newspaper shows:

"On Monday, October 16, Senator Douglas, by appointment, ad- dressed a large audience at Peoria. When he closed he was greeted with six hearty cheers; and the band in attendance played a stirring air. The crowd then began to call for Lincoln, who, as Judge Douglas had announced, was, by agreement, to answer him. Mr. Lincoln then took the stand, and said

"'I do not arise to speak now, if I can stipulate with the audience to meet me here at half past six or at seven o'clock. It is now several minutes past five, and Judge Douglas has spoken over three hours. If you hear me at all, I wish you to hear me thro'. It will take me as long as it has taken him. That will carry us beyond eight o'clock at night. Now every one of you who can remain that long, can just as well get his supper, meet me at seven, and remain one hour or two later. The judge has already informed you that he is to have an hour to reply to me. I doubt not but you have been a little surprised to learn that I have consented to give one of his high reputation and known ability this advantage of me. Indeed, my consenting to it, though reluctant, was not wholly unselfish; for I suspected if it were understood, that the Judge was entirely done, you democrats would leave, and not hear me; but by giving him the close, I felt confident that you would stay for the fun of hearing him skin me.'

"The audience signified their assent to the arrangement, and adjourned to 7 o'clock p. m., at which time they re-assembled, and Mr. Lincoln spoke."Correspondence of the Illinois Journal, Springfield, October 21, 1854.

SENATOR DOUGLAS OF ILLINOIS

The storm center of political agitation, carried to the west of the Alleghany Mountains in the campaign of 1824, gradually advanced with the spread of the people, until the decade between 1850 and 1860 saw it centered in Illinois, mainly through the prominence of Senator Stephen A. Douglas and the Kansas-Nebraska question. As chairman of the Senate Committee on Territories, Douglas fathered and pushed to enactment the famous law of 1854, which repealed the Missouri Compromise so far at it related to the unorganized portion of the Louisi- ana Purchase lying north of 36° 30', and threw it open to slavery or freedom as the future inhabitants might STEPHEN A. DOUGLAS.

From a photograph in the collection of the Illinois Historical Library, supposed to have been made in 1858. determine under the principle of home rule or "popular sovereignty." By this course he brought upon himself the denunciation and abuse of all northern people who opposed the further extension of slave territory.

Immediately upon the adjournment of Congress in August, 1854, Douglas started for Illinois to defend himself before his constituents. Before leaving Washington, he said: "I shall be assailed by demagogues and fanatics there, without stint or moderation. Every opprobrious epithet will be applied to me. I shall probably be hung in effigy in many places. This proceeding may end my political career. But, acting under the sense of duty which animates me, I am prepared to make the sacrifice." He reached Chicago September 2d, and took the rostrum in his own defense at a meeting which he caused to be announced for the following evening. The result may be learned from the newspapers of the day, by reading extracts from writers both favorable and hostile to him.

The Chicago Tribune mentions the following among the occurrences of Friday afternoon:

The flags of all the shipping in port were displayed at half-mast, shortly after noon and remained there during the remainder of the day. At a quarter past six the bells of the city commenced to toll, and commenced to fill the air with their mournful tones for more than an hour. The city wore an air of mourning for the disgrace which her senator was seeking to impose upon her, and which her citizens have determined to resent at any cost.

THE MEETING LAST NIGHT

During the whole of yesterday, the expected meeting of last night was the universal topic of conversation. Crowds of visitors arrived by the special trains from the surrounding cities and towns, even from as far as Detroit and St. Louis, attracted by the announcement that Judge Douglas was to address his constituents.

In consequence of the extreme heat of the weather, it was deemed advisable to hold the meeting on the outside of the hall instead of the inside as had been announced.

At early candle light, a throng of 8,000 persons had assembled at the south part of the North Market Hall.

At the time announced, the Mayor of Chicago called the assemblage to order and Judge Douglas then addressed the meeting..... He was frequently interrupted by the gang of abolition rowdies..... Whenever he approached the subject of the Nebraska bill, an evidently well organized and drilled body of men, comprising about one-twentieth of the meeting, collected and formed into a compact body, refused to allow him to proceed. They kept up this disgraceful proceeding until after ten o'clock.

In vain did the mayor of the city appeal to their sense of order. They refused to let him be heard. Judge Douglas, notwithstanding the uproars of these hirelings, proceeded at intervals.

He told them he was not unprepared for their conduct. He had a day or two since received a letter written by the secretary of an organization framed since his arrival in the city for the purpose of preventing him from speaking. This organization required that he should leave the city or keep silent; and if he disregarded this notice, the organization was pledged at the sacrifice of his life to prevent his being heard. He presented himself, he said, and challenged the armed gang to execute on him their murderous pledge. The letter having been but imperfectly heard, its reading was asked by some of the orderly citizens present, but the mob refused to let it be heard, when Judge Douglas at the earnest request of some of his friends, left the stand.

THE DOUGLAS SPEECH

This grand affair came off Friday night. The St. Louis Republican had made one grand flourish in favor of the immortal Douglas by means of its correspondent, that Douglas would achieve wonders at Chicago and be sustained by the State. Office-holders far and near appeared at Chicago to enjoy his triumph. The evening came, and we will let the Democratic Press speak

Mr. Douglas had a stormy meeting last evening at the North Market Hall. There was a great amount of groans and cheers. But there was nothing like a riot or any approach to it.

He said some bitter things against the press of Chicago, and did not compliment the intelligence of citizens in very pleasant terms. They refused to hear him on these subjects. Towards the close of his speech they became so uproarious that he was obliged to desist.

The plain truth is there were a great many there who were unwilling to hear him and manifested their disapprobation in a very noisy and disrespectful manner. We regret exceedingly that he was not permitted to make his speech unmolested. That would have been far better than the course that was pursued.

We are glad however, that when he decided to make no further efforts the people retired peaceably to their homes and all was quiet.

The Chicago Democrat disposes of the matter even in fewer words:

Senator Douglas. Last evening a large number of citizens assembled in front of the North Market Hall, some to listen to Senator Douglas' remarks on the act known as the Nebraska Act, and some with the express purpose of preventing his making any remarks. The meeting was called to order, and Senator Douglas was introduced to the audience by Mayor Milliken. The noise and disturbance of the audience was such, however, that he was unable to pursue his argument in a manner satisfactory to those who wished to learn what he would say in vindication of his course.

We have heard from private sources that there were ten thousand people present; and that evidently they did not come there to get up a disturbance but simply to demonstrate to Sen. Douglas their opinion of his treachery to his constituents. This they did effectually; and Mr. Douglas now fully understands the estimate in which his conduct is held by his townsmen at Chicago.

It is said that Mr. Douglas felt, intensely, the rebuke he had received.

The office-holders who went to Chicago from here and elsewhere are very quiet on their return, and have learnt something of public opinion in the north part of the state.

SPEECH OF SENATOR DOUGLAS

At the North Market Hall on Friday Evening, September 1st. 1854
You have been told that the bill legislated slavery into territory now free. It docs no such thing. As most of you have never read that bill, I will read to you the fourteenth section. It will be seen that the bill leaves the people perfectly free. It is perfectly natural for those who have misrepresented and slandered me, to be unwilling to hear me. I am here in my own home.

I am in my own home, and have lived in Illinois long before you thought of the State. I know my rights, and, though personal violence has been threatened me, I am determined to maintain them. The principle of the Nebraska bill grants to the people of the territories the right to govern themselves. Who dares deny that right. What is the Missouri Compromise line? It was simply a line, recognizing slavery on one side of it and forbidding it on the other. Now would any of you permit the establishment of slavery on either side of any line?

Mr. Douglas said he would show that all of his audience were in 1S4S in favor of the repeal of the Missouri Compromise and he alone was opposed to it.

The compromise measures of 1850 were endorsed by our own city Council. They were also endorsed by our legislature almost unanimously. The resolution passed by our Legislature in 1851, approved of the principles of non-intervention, in the most direct and strongest terms. All the Representatives except four whigs voted for the resolution.Every representative from Cook county voted for them.

These were the instructions under which he acted. Till then he was the fast friend of the Compromise. Simply because another principle had been adopted and I acted upon that principle.

The question now became more frequent and the people more noisy. Judge

Douglas became excited, and said many things not very creditable to his position and character. The people as a consequence refused to hear him further, and although he kept the stand for a considerable time he was obliged at last to give way and retire to his lodgings at the Tremont House. The people then separated quietly and all except the office-holders, in the greatest of good humor.

A large number, and we certainly were among them, felt deeply mortified that Mr. Douglas had not been permitted to say what he pleased. We must say, however, that the matter terminated much more peacefully than most of our citizens feared, and all have reason, considering the excited state of public mind, to be thankful that matters are no worse.

ABRAHAM LINCOLN OF ILLINOIS

Among those who opposed the action of Douglas was his long-time friend and rival, Abraham Lincoln, who had served several terms in the Illinois State Legislature and one term in Congress (1847-49) and then retired from public life to look after his law practice. After six years of retirement, he confessed himself drawn again into the arena of politics by the passing of the Kansas-Nebraska act. In the dissatisfaction with Douglas and the Democratic dissension likely to follow, Lincoln saw an opportunity for the Whigs of Illinois and an opening for his long-suppressed political ambitions. During the autumn of 1854, after Douglas had been refused a hearing in Chicago, Lincoln wrote to an influential friend, "It has come around that a Whig may by possibility be elected to the United States Senate, and I want the chance of being that man."

At this time, Lincoln was among the most prominent of the old line Whigs of Illinois; but the dissensions in the Democratic party which promised him a hearing also brought an obstacle in the many prominent Democrats who were deserting the pro-slavery Douglas and who might properly be called new line Whigs, although known as anti-Nebraska men. The Whigs, never able to carry the state, welcomed an alliance with these seceders on the common basis of opposition to slavery extension; naturally a greater public interest would attach to them than to a regular Whig like Lincoln; and the latter was in danger of being relegated to second place during the important Springfield Fair week of 1854.

Heretofore the Democracy of Central and Southern Illinois, who disagree with Judge Douglas on the Nebraskan measure, have been almost entirely silent in regard to it, and Judge Douglas and his supporters in the matter have had matters entirely their own way.... This state of things, as every one must have foreseen, could not last long. The democracy have been aroused

35

and Judge Douglas is to be met at Springfield by several of the first minds of the State, men who would honor any State or nation and no less giants than himself. We are informed that Judge Trumbull, Judge Breese, Col. McClernand Judge Palmer, Col. E. D. Taylor, and others will be there and reply to Judge Douglas. He will find as foemen tried Democrats, lovers of the Baltimore platform and opposed to all slavery agitationgiants in intellect, worthy of his steel.

THE DEBATES OF 1854

The Illinois State Agricultural Fair held annually at Springfield was the culminating political event of the yeara characteristic which it bears to the present day. This gathering, devoted primarily to the interests of the farmer, became a rendezvous for state politicians, where plans were laid, candidates brought out, and the issues of the day discussed by the ablest speakers in each party. Douglas well knew that he must defend himself against the Whigs and also against many former supporters in his own party, as indicated in the quotation above. Leaving Chicago after failing to secure a hearing, Douglas went to Indianapolis and then returned to Illinois, addressing enthusiastic meetings at Ottawa, Joliet, Rock Island, and other places before the first week in October, which was the date of the State Fair. Springfield at this time contained about fifteen thousand inhabitants and the visitors to the fair increased the population at least ten thousand. It was the day of stump speaking. The farmers held sessions daily during the week at which they discussed topics pertaining to agriculture and its allied interests; each evening a woman was lecturing in the court room on "Woman's Influence in the Great Progressive Movements of the Day;" and the politicians occupied the senate chamber from noon to midnight with a short intermission for supper. In a card given out through the press, the members of the Agricultural Society protested against the political speakers taking advantage of their "Annual Jubilee and School of Life" to occupy the time and distract the attention of the people by a public discussion of questions foreign to the objects of the society. "The politicians as well as the farmers are out in force," wrote a reporter.

On Wednesday of Fair week, Douglas spoke in the Hall of Representatives in the State House, making a masterly defense of himself and his theory of popular sovereignty. He was to be answered at the same place the following afternoon by Judge Trumbull, of Alton, the most prominent anti-Nebraska Democrat in the southern part of the state. Trumbull failed to arrive at the proper time and Abraham Lincoln, a Whig, arose to reply to Douglas. Lincoln was the recognized speaker for the Whigs in Springfield: a month before, he had replied to Calhoun, a pro-Nebraska Democrat.

POLITICAL SPEAKING

Today we listened to a 3+1/2 hour's speech from the Hon. Abram Lincoln, in reply to that of Judge Douglas of yesterday. He made a full and convincing reply and showed up squatter sovereignty in all its unblushing pretensions. We came away as Judge Douglas commenced to reply to Mr. Lincoln.

LINCOLN AT THE STATE FAIR

My acquaintance with Mr. Lincoln began in October, 1854. I was then in the employ of the Chicago Evening Journal. I had been sent to Springfield to report the political doings of State Fair week for that newspaper. Thus it came about that I occupied a front seat in the Representatives' Hall, in the old State House when Mr. Lincoln delivered a speech already described in this volume. The impression made upon me by the orator was quite overpowering. I had not heard much political speaking up to that time. I have heard a great deal since. I have never heard anything since, either by Mr. Lincoln, or by anybody, that I would put on a higher plane of oratory. All the strings that play upon the human heart and understanding were touched with masterly skill and force, while beyond and above all skill was the overwhelming conviction pressed upon the audience that the speaker himself was charged with an irresistible and inspiring duty to his fellowmen.....

Although I heard him many times afterward, I shall longest remember him as I then saw the tall, angular form with the long, angular arms, at times bent nearly double with excitement, like a large flail animating two smaller ones, the mobile face wet with perspiration which he discharged in drops as he threw his head this way and that like a projectilenot a graceful figure and yet not an ungraceful one.

Lincoln spoke until half-past five; Douglas replied for an hour and then announced that he would leave off to enable the listeners to have their suppers and would resume at early candle light. But when that time arrived, Douglas for some reason failed to resume, other speakers took the platform, and Douglas' "unfinished speech" was the cause of endless raillery on the part of the Whigs who claimed that he found Lincoln's arguments unanswerable. The style of argument of each was known to the other because they had debated public questions in Springfield as early as seventeen years before. Trumbull arrived in time to speak on Thursday evening and his speech was widely copied in the press of the state as representative anti-Nebraska doctrine. Lincoln, through the influence of his friend Herndon, was given extravagant praise in the Journal of Springfield, but his speech created no widespread comment throughout the state such as Herndon would have us believe.

HON. A. LINCOLN'S SPEECH

Agreeably to previous notice, circulated in the morning by hand bill, Hon. A. Lincoln delivered a speech yesterday, at the State House, in the Hall of Representatives in reply to the speech of Senator Douglas, of the preceding day. Mr. L. commenced at 2 o'clock, p. m., and spoke above three hours, to a very large, intelligent and attentive audience. Judge Douglas had been invited by Mr. Lincoln to be present and to reply to Mr. Lincoln's remarks, if he should think proper to do so. And Judge Douglas was present, and heard Mr. Lincoln throughout.

Mr. Lincoln closed amid immense cheers. He had nobly and triumphantly sustained the cause of a free people, and won a place in their hearts as a bold and powerful champion of equal rights for American citizens, that will in all time be a monument to his honor. Mr. Douglas replied to Mr. Lincoln, in a speech of about two hours. It was adroit, and plausible, but had not the marble of logic in it.

LINCOLN AND DOUGLAS

The debate between these two men came off in the State House on the fifth of October. The Hall of the House of Representatives in which the speaking was heard, was crowded to overflowing. The number present was about two thousand, Mr. Lincoln commenced at 2 o'clock p. m., and spoke three hours and ten minutes.

We propose to give our views and those of many northerners and many southerners upon the debate. We intend to give it as fairly as we can. Those who know Mr. Lincoln, know him to be a conscien- tious and honest man, who makes no assertions that he does not know to be true.

It was a proud day for Lincoln. His friends will never forget it. The news had gone abroad that "Lincoln was afraid to meet Douglas;" but when he arose, his manly and fearless form shut up and crushed out the charge. We will not soon forget his appearance as he bowed to the audience, and looked over the vast sea of human heads.

Douglas arose and commenced his answers to Mr. Lincolnand his eloquence can only be compared to his personfalse and brusque. He is haughty and imperative,his voice somewhat shrill and his manner positive;now flattering, now wild with excess of madness That trembling fore-finger, like a lash, was his whip to drive the doubting into the ranks. He is a very tyrant.

When he arose he most evidently was angry for being bearded in the Capitol, and if we judge not wrongly, we affirm that he is conscious of his ruin and doom. The marks and evidences of desolation are furrowed in his face, written on his brow.

Lincoln next followed Douglas to Peoria and replied to him at that point, October 16, 1854. A fortnight later elections were held for members of the state legislature who would choose in joint session a fellow-senator for

Douglas from Illinois.

SENATORIAL ELECTION OF 1854

The legislative elections proved unfortunate for the indorsement of Douglas and brought a large number of anti-Nebraska men into the joint assembly. It seemed that Lincoln's senatorial aspirations were in a fair way to be realized; but at the last moment it was found necessary to elect Judge Trumbull, an anti-Nebraska Democrat, to prevent the choice falling upon Governor Matteson, who was not sound on opposition to the extension of slavery in Kansas.

SENATORIAL ELECTION

Trumbull ElectedThe Anti-Nebraska Sentiment of Illinois Vindicated
The Senatorial election took place on yesterday..... Abraham Lincoln had by far the largest number of votes on the first votes: but it having become apparent that he could not be elected, his friends to a man, with his entire approbation, united on a candidate that could be, and was, elected. Every vote Judge Trumbull received came from anti-Nebraska and anti-Douglas men. Thus has the State of Illinois rebuked the authors of the repeal of the Missouri restriction.They have done it in a manner that will be felt, not only in this State, but throughout the nation. The Douglas party would have greatly preferred the election of Lincoln, Williams, Odgen, Kellogg, or Sweet, to that of Judge Trumbull. They were most anxious to crush him for daring to be honest.
Of Mr. Lincoln, we need scarcely say,that though ambitious of the office himself,when it was apparent that he could not be elected, he pressed his friends to vote for Mr. Trumbull.Mr. Lincoln's friends can well say, that while with his advice they ultimately cast their votes for, and assisted in the election of Mr. Trumbull, it was not "because they loved Ceasar less, but because they loved Rome more."
It has long been certain that there was an anti-Nebraska majority in the Legislature. The Douglas men were certain of this factand their anticipated "triumph," as announced by Mr. Moulton in the House, was based on the known popularity of Gov. Matteson personally, which would give their votes for him and which would ensure his election.
Although Herndon and Lincoln's other friends attempted in these complimentary terms to soften the blow of his defeat, he felt keenly the sacrifice he had been compelled to make for a man who had been until recently his political enemy, "I regret my defeat moderately," he wrote to a

friend, "but am not nervous about it." Quite naturally he would be given a chance when the next senatorial vacancy occurred and that would be four years hence.

PRESIDENTIAL ELECTION OF 1856

As the presidential year of 1856 came on, the old line Whigs and anti-Nebraska men were fused into the new Republican party through spontaneous conventions held in the different northern states. In Illinois, "People's" conventions assembled in the counties and named delegates to a state convention which was held in Bloomington in May, representing "those regardless of party who oppose the further extension of slave territory and who wish to curb the rising pretentions of the slave oligarchy." Among the prominent men present was Abraham Lincoln, who spoke at the close of the convention. Reporters afterward testified that the spell of his simple oratory was so entrancing that they forgot their tasks and the speech went unreported. In later years it was written out from memory by one of the hearers and became known as "Lincoln's lost speech," being the subject of no little controversy.

HON. A. LINCOLN

During the recent session of the State anti-Nebraska Convention, the Hon. A. Lincoln of this city made one of the most powerful and convincing speeches which we have ever heard. The editor of the Chicago Press, thus characterizes it:

Abram Lincoln of Springfield was next called out, and made the speech of the occasion. Never has it been our fortune to listen to a more eloquent and masterly presentation of a subject. I shall not mar any of its fine proportions or brilliant passages by attempting even a synopsis of it. Mr. Lincoln must write it out and let it go before all the people. For an hour and a half he held the assemblage spell-bound by the power of his argument, the intense irony of his invective, and the deep earnestness and fervid brilliancy of his eloquence. When he concluded, the audience sprang to their feet, and cheer after cheer told how deeply their hearts had been touched, and their souls warmed up to a generous enthusiasm.

In the Democratic national convention which met at Cincinnati, June 2, 1856, Douglas on one ballot received 121 votes, but the nomination eventually went to James Buchanan. In the Republican national convention, which met at Philadelphia, two weeks later, Lincoln was given 110 votes on the informal vote for the vice-presidency, but Dayton was nominated. Lincoln headed the list of Illinois electors for Fremont and Dayton. During the campaign, Douglas took the stump for Buchanan and Lincoln for Fremont. After the defeat of Fremont, Lincoln said in a speech at a banquet in Chicago: "In the late contest we were divided between Fremont and Buchanan. Can we not come together in the future? Let bygones be bygones; let past differences be as nothing; and with steady eye on the real issue, let us re-inaugurate the good old 'central ideas' of the republic. We can do it. The human heart is with us; God is with us."

In June, of the following year, 1857, Douglas spoke in Springfield on current political topics and two weeks later Lincoln answered him at the same place.

CHAPTER II. THE SENATORIAL CAMPAIGN OF 1858

Douglas was chosen to the United States Senate from Illinois for the first time in 1847 and was re-elected in 1853; consequently his second term would expire in 1859 and he must at that time seek a new election at the hands of the Illinois legislature. To compass this end, he must control the legislative elections of 1858. The state was never lost to the Democratic column before 1860; but Douglas found himself obliged to enter the campaign of 1858 under peculiar and embarrassing circumstances. The plan by which he had hoped to establish home rule in Kansas had caused a situation in the territory which bade fair to test the principle of "popular sovereignty" and to create dissension in the Democratic party. Some of the residents of the territory late in 1857 framed and adopted a constitution at Lecompton; but the free-soil people of the territory refused to take part in the proceedings. The adoption by Congress of this "Lecompton constitution" was favored by President Buchanan, but was opposed by Senator Douglas on the ground that it was not a fair test of "popular sovereignty." If Douglas were successful in securing a re-election in Illinois, it could be interpreted in no other way than a defeat for the administration and an invitation to other ambitious statesmen to brook presidential disfavor. It was reported that Buchanan warned Douglas of his peril and that Douglas replied, "Mr. President, Andrew Jackson is dead," implying that the days of presidential dictation were past. Consequently the new Republican party of Illinois had an unexpected opportunity of aiding a Democratic president to defeat a Democratic senator for re-election.

If Douglas entered the canvass beset with difficulty, Lincoln was far from being able to place the contest purely on the basis of merit. The patronage of the state so long enjoyed by Senator Douglas under Democratic administration had dotted the state with Douglas postmasters, revenue collectors, and other federal officers. That Lincoln fully appreciated this handicap is evident from one of his Springfield speeches of 1858:

"Senator Douglas is of world-wide renown. All the anxious politicians of his party, or who have been of his party for years past, have been looking upon him as certainly, at no distant day, to be the president of the United States. They have seen in his round, jolly, fruitful face, post-offices, land-offices, marshallships, and cabinet appointments, chargeships and foreign missions, bursting and sprouting out in wonderful exuberance, ready to be laid hold of by their greedy hands. And as they have been gazing upon this attractive picture so long, they cannot, in the little distraction that has taken place in the party, bring themselves to give up the charming hope: but with greedier anxiety they rush about him, sustain him, and give him marches, triumphant entries, and receptions beyond what even in the days of his highest prosperity they could have brought about in his favor.

"On the contrary, nobody has ever expected me to be president. In my poor, lean, lank face, nobody has ever seen that any cabbages were sprouting out. These are disadvantages all, taken together, that the Republicans labor under. We have to fight this battle upon principle, and upon principles alone."

There was also a possibility that at the last moment it might become necessary to name as the Republican candidate for the senatorship a former Democrat, as had been done in the election of 1854. It was also rumored that John Wentworth of Chicago was the real candidate and THE OLD STATE HOUSE, SPRINGFIELD, ILLINOIS that Lincoln was to be used as a stalking-horse for the defeat of Douglas in the legislative campaign.

Mr. A. Lincoln is the special object of admiration among the Black Republicans of Illinois at this time. How long it will last no one knows. Two years ago he occupied much the same position, but he was diddled out of the place of Senator by the friends of Trumbull, and the same thing may happen to him again.

Lincoln's prospects for the senatorship were further menaced by the danger that the Republicans of the state might deem it wise to lend their support to Douglas, reelect him to the Senate, and by his victory impair the chances of Buchanan securing a second term. Greeley suggested that the Illinois senatorship should be allowed to go to Douglas by default and thus by increasing the breach between Douglas and Buchanan prepare the way for the Republicans to carry the state in 1860. Lincoln himself expressed his fears lest Douglas should shift from his true Democratic principles, and "assume steep Free Soil ground and furiously assail the Administration on the stump." This very possible action would take away the support of the anti-Nebraska Democrats and of many Republicans from Lincoln and center it on the Little Giant. Against such a coalition Lincoln took the precaution of sending letters to prominent Republicans throughout the state, before the Republican convention met at Springfield in June, 1858, and they soon acknowledged the danger of indorsing so uncertain a man as Douglas upon no other recommendation to Republicanism than his quarrel with Buchanan. The situation might be foreguarded if the Republican convention would indorse Lincoln as its candidate, thereby pledging the legislators elected on its ticket in the November election to vote for Lincoln in the joint session to be held during the winter of 1859.

REPUBLICAN STATE CONVENTION OF ILLINOIS

Great Harmony and Enthusiasm

B. C. Cooke, of LaSalle, offered the following resolution which was unanimously adopted:

Resolved: That the Hon. Lyman Trumbull in the Senate of the United States has illustrated and defined the principles of the Republican party with distinguished ability and fidelity, and we hereby express our emphatic approval of his course.

Chas. L. Wilson, of Cook, submitted the following resolution, which was greeted with shouts of applause and unanimously adopted:

Resolved: That Abraham Lincoln is the first and only choice of the Republicans of Illinois for the United States Senate, as the successor of Stephen A. Douglas.

On motion, the Convention adjourned to meet at 8 o'clock.

8 o'clock p. m.

Convention met, pursuant to adjournment.

Resolutions complimentary to the officers of the State government, and also to the officers of the Convention were unanimously adopted.

Speeches were made by Hon. Abraham Lincoln, T. J. Turner, I. N, Arnold, J. J. Feree, C. B. Denio, Wyche, Hopkins and others, and the Convention adjourned with long and hearty cheers for the ticket and the cause.

(Signed) Gustavus Koerner, Pres't.

D. M. Whitney, etc., Vice Pres'ts.

W. H. Bailhache, etc., Sec'ies.

REPUBLICAN STATE TICKET

For State Treasurer
JAMES MILLER
of McLean County

For Superintendent of Public Instruction
NEWTON BATEMAN
of Morgan County

THE REPUBLICAN CONVENTION

About seven o'clock, the Convention adjourned to meet in the evening; but previous to doing so, an incident occured worthy of notice. The delegates from Cook county appeared with a banner upon which was inscribed, "Cook county for Abram Lincoln for United States Senator." Mr. Judd, of Cook, in a very appropriate address referred to this fact, when a delegate in the crowd arose, and, waving a flag on which was printed the word "Illinois," moved that it be nailed over "Cook county" in the banner carried by the Cook delegation. The motion was received with rounds of applause, and carried by a unanimous vote. The inscription then read ILLINOIS FOR ABRAM LINCOLN FOR U. S. Senator

In the evening, the Hall was again crowded to excess to listen to the speeches from Lincoln, Judd, Wyche, Feree, Denio, and others. It would take up more room and time than are at our disposal to comment upon the speeches delivered, and the unbounded enthusiasm which prevailed.

LINCOLN AT THE REPUBLICAN STATE CONVENTION

Returning to the campaign of 1858 I was sent by my employers to Springfield to attend the Republican State Convention of that year. Again I sat at a short distance from Mr. Lincoln when he delivered the "House-divided-against-itself" speech on the 17th of June. This was delivered from manuscript and was the only one I ever heard him deliver in that way. When it was concluded he put the manuscript in my hands and asked me to go to the State Journal office and read the proof of it. I think it had already been set in type. Before I had finished this task, Mr. Lincoln himself came into the composing room of the State Journal and looked over the revised proofs. He said to me that he had taken a great deal of pains with this speech, and that he wanted it to go before the people just as he had prepared it. He dded that some of his friends had scolded him a good deal about the opening paragraph and "the house divided against itself," and wanted him to change it or to leave it out altogether, but that he believed he had studied this subject more deeply than they had, and that he was going to stick to that text whatever happened.

ALL FOR LINCOLN

During the progress of the convention on yesterday, the Chicago delegation brought in a banner with the motto upon it "Cook County is for Abraham Lincoln." It was received with shouts and hurrahs of the most vociferous character. On motion of one of the Peoria delegates, the motto was amended to read"Illinois Is for Abraham Lincoln," which brought down the House with three times three and three extra.Springfield Journal.

The Republican enemies of Long John in Chicago thought they had put a nail in his coffin by preparing this banner, and the result is that they think they have effectually killed off his Senatorial aspirations by the above proceeding. Another move is to nominate E. Peck and Kriessman for the legislature from North Chicago, and Meech and Scripps from South Chicago. We'll see if Long John is to be beaten or not.

It was now less than two years until the Republicans would nominate a candidate for the presidency. That Lincoln was not regarded as a possibility even in Illinois is shown by the following:

Vote on the Presidency.The vote among the Republican Delegates to the Illinois State Convention and passengers on the morning train, indicating their preference for the Presidency, stood as follows:

William H. Seward

139

S. P. Chase

6

John C. Freemont

32

W. H. Bissell
2

John McLean
13
Scattering
26

Lyman Trumbull
7

The speech in which Lincoln acknowledged the courtesy of the convention was thought out in advance and every sentence carefully weighed. It marked the new lines upon which Lincoln proposed to argue the situation and which ultimately won success. Boldly casting aside the long-prevalent idea that the Union could be saved by compromise and by repressing agitation, Lincoln voiced the new opinion in a slightly altered Scriptural quotation, "A house divided against itself cannot stand. " He declared that the government could not endure permanently half slave and half free; it must become all one thing or all the other. Whether Lincoln foresaw that the astute Douglas would construe this statement into a desire to dissolve the Union is a matter of doubt, as is also the question whether he appreciated the danger that his criticism of the Dred Scott decision would be twisted by Douglas into a revolutionary attack on the Supreme Court.

Since the campaign was to be waged against Senator Douglas, Lincoln devoted a large part of his speech to showing the unfitness of the Illinois senator to lead Republicans in their attempt to check the growing territorial power of the slaveholding dynasty, and to ridiculing the pretended greatness of the senator. "They remind us," said he, "that he is a great man and that the largest of us are very small ones. Let that be granted. But 'a living dog is better than a dead lion.' Judge Douglas, if not a dead lion, for his work, is at least a caged and toothless one. How can he oppose the advances of slavery? He don't care about it..... But clearly, he is not now with ushe does not pretend to behe does not promise ever to be." He insinuated that the Dred Scott decision was a part of a Democratic programme. "We cannot absolutely know," said he, "that all these exact adaptations are the result of preconcert. But when we see a lot of framed timbers, different portions of which we know have been gotten out at different times and places by different workmenStephen, Franklin, Roger, and James, for instanceand we see these timbers joined together, and see them exactly make the frame of a house or mill, all the tenons and mortises exactly fitting and all the lengths and proportions of the different pieces exactly adapted to their respective places, and not a piece too many or too few, not omitting even scaffoldingor, if a single piece be lacking, we see the place in the frame exactly fitted and prepared yet to bring such piece inin such a case we find it impossible not to believe that Stephen and Franklin and Roger and James all understood one another from the beginning, and all worked upon a common plan or draft drawn up before the first blow was struck."

THE DOUGLAS BOLTERS

The breach between Douglas and the administration was reflected in the Democratic state convention which met at Springfield, April 21, 1858. As soon as resolutions were introduced approving the course of Senator Douglas, a considerable number of delegates withdrew from the convention and formed a "rump" assembly in another room. They were mostly from Chicago and the northern part of the state. These "bolters" called another convention which met at Springfield, June 9, nominated candidates, and adopted resolutions denouncing Douglas and characterizing his opposition to the administration on the Lecompton question as "an act of overweening conceit."

THE BOLTERS CONVENTION

In another column we publish the telegraphic report of the proceedings of the Bolters Convention at Springfield yesterday. It was a miserable farce. It is represented that 48 of the 100 counties were represented, and considering that the delegates were self-appointed, and that offices under the federal government were promised to all who would attend, the fact that in 52 counties there could not be found men mean enough to participate in the proceedings, is a glorious tribute to the fidelity of the Democracy of Illinois. Dougherty and Reynolds were nominated, and if they receive 2,500 votes in the whole State it will astonish even themselves.

We publish also the letter of our correspondent detailing the events of Tuesdaythe drunken orgies of the men, who, rioting on the public money, have been a disgrace to the State, to the party and now even to themselves.

SONG OF THE HYENAS

The following, which we clip from an eastern contemporary, is entitled "Senator Douglas and His Persecutors, or, the Battle Song of the Hyenas." It undoubtedly contains "more truth than poetry," and we cordially commend it to the careful perusal of the Illinois Danites:

1.

We'll hunt the lion down,
We jolly bold Hyenas,
Though honest folks may think
We're just about as mean as

2.

The devils are, who make
Poor bigots torture people,
Because the people can't
Uphold said bigots' steeple,

3.

O won't it be such fun
To crush the "Little Giant"
Who, conscious of the right,
Is saucy and defiant?

4.

Why can't he do like us
Stoop low for place and plunder?
Such independence does
Excite our wrath and wonder.

5.

Of course in open day
We never will attack him,
For then his voice would call
The masses up to back him;

6.

But at the midnight hour
In dark and gloomy weather,
In some old grave-yard foul,
We'll congregate together.

7.

And lay secret plan
To stuff with spoils our leanness;
And hunting Douglas down
Will gratify our meanness!

Although these "bolters" represented fewer than half the counties of the state, their action was significant and the contagion might spread. Consequently, one week later Douglas turned aside in the Senate from the pending question upon which he was speaking to address his fellow senator's on the condition of political parties in Illinois. In a speech characteristically abusive he denounced the leader of the "bolters" as an ex-Mormon with an unwholesome record, and he fastened upon the recalcitrants the name of "Danite," by which they were known during the remainder of the campaign. He took care during the course of his remarks to state that in his opinion Buchanan was not a party to the attacks made upon him from the ranks in Illinois.

The Democratic press of the state immediately lined up with the rival conventions. A majority of the editors of the state favored Douglas, who had thus far been intrusted with a large part of the federal patronage of the state. The Whig editors took no part in the quarrel; the Buchananites were sadly in the minority. Some of the Douglas supporters went so far as to place the name of Douglas at the head of a column on the editorial page, as if the election of a senator were to be determined by popular vote. This, added to the direct nomination of Lincoln by the Republican convention, gave additional color to the popular aspect of the campaign. It was as if the two were running for the presidency rather than for an election to a senatorship through a state legislature.

Mr. Lincoln is recommended for Senator and however unusual such an issue may be, it is now plainly and squarely one before the people of the State for United States senatorStephen A. Douglas on the one side and Abraham Lincoln of the other; the Democracy of the one against the black republican principles of the other.

ILLINOIS

Sketch of the Hon. Abraham Lincoln Correspondence of the New York Tribune

Collinsville, Ill., June 15, 1858
The decided expressions of the Republican Convention of this State in favor of Abraham Lincoln for Senator, in the place now held by Judge Douglas, will give interest to anything throwing light upon the character and abilities of Mr. Lincoln, especially to those who are not acquainted with him. As he has served only one term in the Lower House of Congress, and that so long ago as 1846-8, there must be many who would like to know how he will be likely to fill the place of the now so notoriousI might say distinguishedDouglas. Is he a match for his "illustrious predecessor"?
But I am forgetting myself, which was chiefly to relate an incident showing the two men in contact and somewhat in comparsion. I think it has never been in print.
It was in the Fall of 1854, when the Nebraska bill was a fresh topic, Lincoln was speaking to some two thousand persons in the State House at Springfield. Douglas sat on the Clerk's platform, just under the Speaker's stand. In his introduction, Lincoln complimented his distinguished friend; said he himself had not been in public life as he had; and if he should, on that account, misstate any fact, he would be very much obliged to his friend the Judge, if he would correct him. Judge Douglas rose with a good deal of Senatorial dignity, and said that it was not always agreeable to a speaker to be interrupted in the course of his remarks, and therefore, if he should have anything to say, he would wait until Mr. Lincoln was done. For some reason, he did not keep to his purpose, but quite frequently rose to put in a word when he seemed to think his case required immediate attention. One

of these passagesand it was pretty nearly a sample of the restwas in this wise: Lincoln had been giving a history of the legislation of the Federal Government on the subject of Slavery, and referring to the opinions held by public men, and had come down to the Nicholson letter, wherein the denial of the power of Congress to prohibit Slavery in the Territories was first presented to the public. Said he, "I don't know what my friend the Judge thinks" [and he looked down upon him with a smile half playful, half roguish], "but really it seems to me that that was the origin of the Nebraska bill." This stroke at the Senator's laurels in the matter of the "great principle," created a good deal of laughter and some applause, which brought the Judge to his feet. Shaking back his heavy hair, and looking much like a roused lion, he said, in his peculiarly heavy voice which he uses with so much effect when he wishes to be impressive, "No, Sir! I will tell you what was the origin of the Nebraska bill. It was this, Sir! God created man, and placed before him both good and evil, and left him free to choose for himself. That was the origin of the Nebraska bill." As he said this, Lincoln looked the picture of good nature and patience. As Douglas concluded, the smile which lurked in the corners of Lincoln's mouth parted his lips, and he replied, "Well, then, I think it is a great honor to Judge Douglas that he was the first man to discover that fact." This brought down the house, of course, but I could not perceive that the Judge appreciated the fun in the least... W.

Congress adjourned June 1, 1858, and Douglas started for Chicago by way of northern New York, where he intended paying a visit to his aged mother. So prominently before the public was he at this time, in view of the coming contest in Illinois, that the newspapers chronicled his every movement on the way.

SENATOR DOUGLAS

Senator Douglas, accompanied by his beautiful and accomplished wife, arrived at the Girard House, Monday night, from Washington en route for Chicago, where he proposes opening his campaign.He was visited, in the course of yesterday, by a large number of our most influential citizens holding quite an impromptu levee, in fact, for no special announcement of his arrival in this city had been made. He appeared in excellent health and spirits. He left New York by the afternoon train.Phila. Press.

Senator Douglas is at present at his mother's in the State of New Yorkrecruiting previous to entering upon the campaign in this State It is said that he will open the ball at Carlinville, Macoupin County.

Col. Carpenter on the part of the Administration Democrats, is to take the stump, it is said, and meet Douglas in the field.

The Republican standard bearer will be Hon. Abe Lincolnand we could not place our cause in abler hands.

Let the people hear and judge between the principles of these con- tending parties.

MR. DOUGLAS IN ILLINOIS

The Dismantled Democracy and the Administration

We have been informed, from a satisfactory source, that it is the purpose of Mr. Senator Douglas (now en route homeward) to enter at once upon the state campaign of Illinois, which, in the approaching fall election, is to determine the complexion of the Legislature, and thus whether Mr. Douglas or some other man is, for the next term of six years, to take the chair so long occupied in the United States Senate by the "Little Giant." We learn, too, that adopting a conciliatory course toward the administration, the plan of the campaign of Mr. Douglas will be war to the knife against the destructive antislavery heresies of the late Illinois State Convention, and of their Senatorial nominee, Mr. Lincoln; and that thus, taking up the glove thrown before him, Mr. Douglas, upon the broad democratic principles of constitutional obligations and state rights, will make a fair field fight with the opposition upon the ground of their own choosing.

In this aspect of affairs, the Illinois Republicans having coolly turned their backs upon Mr. Douglas, he is in an excellent position to understand the exact necessities of his case, the difficulties of his party and the way to surmount them.

Considering, therefore, the dangers which surround the Illinois Democracy, with the critical position of Mr. Douglas on the one hand, and the excessive confidence of the opposition on the other, we may anticipate a campaign out there as desperate as that of the Pennsylvania October election of 1856, and perhaps as momentous to the Democratic party in reference to the Presidency.

ILLINOIS POLITICS

A correspondent, a particular friend and admirer of Douglas, writing from Olney, Ill., under date of July 3d, to the Vincennes Sun, gives a glimpse of the fight in Illinois.

The Little Giant will soon be among us, and as he moves about we can tell how the people feel. It is conceded here that it's all right in this district.

Every district where there is any hope will be looked after and nothing left undone that will tend to success. By about September the whole state will be alive with stumpers,Douglas will be backed by the "giants," and the Black Republican Ajaxes will be in the field armed for the conflict. Distintinguished speakers from all parts of the Union on both sides are promised.

Lincoln is popularthe strongest man the opposition have,is nearly fifty years oldsix feet twoslightly stoop-shoulderedvery muscular and powerfuldark eyesa quizzical, pleasant, raw-boned facetells a a story better than anybody elseis a good lawyerand is what the world calls a devilish good fellow.He would have been senator before, had not Trumbull's superior cunning overreached him. But, in dignity, intellect and majesty of mind it is not pretended that he is Douglas's equal.

MR. DOUGLAS HIS PASSAGE THROUGH OHIO HIS COMFORTERS

The Honorable Stephen A. Douglas appears to have put himself into not very desirable hands in his passage through the state of Ohio. It is true that if he found it advisable to put himself into any hands whatever, he had left to him very little freedom of choice. The original Buchanan men, and those whose interests it is still to appear to cling to the presidential faction, could not, of course, have anything to do with him.

Having addressed a large gathering of the people at Clifton Springs, N. Y., on the Fourth of July, Douglas departed for Chicago. In New York, at Cleveland, and at Toledo, Ohio, he was tendered serenades and receptions. Recalling the unfortunate manner in which the people of Chicago had greeted him four years before, his supporters now planned a reception which, by its very magnitude would overwhelm hostility if any were manifest and would also show Buchanan that Illinois chose to follow her senator rather than the President. It was the first of the extraordinary rallies made to the banner of Douglas in the campaign of 1858.

(From the Chicago Times of Saturday, 10th)

SENATOR DOUGLAS AT HOME

As per announcement in the programme of the reception of Hon. Stephen A. Douglas, published by authority of the committee of arrangements, an extra train of cars was ready at 1 o'clock, yesterday, to convey the committee of reception to Michigan Citydistant from Chicago sixty milesat which place Senator Douglas was to take the Illinois Central road on the return trip.

In the meantime, also, a great number of national flags were being elevated at conspicuous points near the depot and elsewhere, and banners of different shapes and colors, besides streamers, pennants, etc., were disposed in all directions.

It was now 1 o'clock. The train was to start at that hour, and all things being ready, the cars moved off amid shouts from the outside, and answering shouts and music from within. In all the company numbered four hundred. A splendid banner, that of the young Men's Democratic Club, was carried upon the locomotive.

The train proceeded to Michigan City, where it was met by a host of gallant Indianians, who accompanied the Judge from Laporte to Michigan City. Some malicious person having secretly spiked the only gun in the town, the democracy obtained a large anvil, and placing it in the middle of the street, made the welkin echo with its repeated discharges.

THE RETURN TO THE CITY

At a few minutes after five o'clock the procession was formed and proceeded to the depot. Judge Douglas being now the guest of the committee. The train soon started, and all along the roadat every station, at almost every farmhouse and laborer's cabinin every cornfield and at every point where laborers were engagedthere was

exhibited by cheers, by waving of handkerchiefs and other demonstrations, that cordial "welcome home" to the great representative of popular rights.

At the outer depot of the Illinois Central railroad the national flag had been raised by the operatives, and a swivel belched forth its roaring notes of welcome. The hardy hands of the mechanics resounded with applause, and cheers and huzzas continued until the train had passed on to the city.

As the train passed along from Twelfth street to the depot, crowds of ladies were assembled on the doorsteps of the residences on Michigan avenue, waving banners and handkerchiefs; the lake part was crowded by persons hastily proceeding to the depot. Long before the train could enter the station house, thousands had crossed over the breakwater, got upon the track, and climbed into the cars, and when the latter reached the depot they were literally crammed inside and covered on top by ardent and enthusiastic friends and supporters of the illustrious Illinoisan.

Capt. Smith's artillery were, in the meantime, firing from Dearborn Park a salute of 150 guns, (guns were also firing in the west and north divisions) the booming of the cannon alone rising above the cheering plaudits of the assembled multitude. The hotels and principal buildings of the city were adorned with flags.

The Adams House, near the Central depot, was most handsomely decorated. The national flag, a banner bearing the motto "Douglas, the champion of Popular Sovereignty," as well as numerous flags belonging to vessels in the harbor were suspended across the street, presenting a grand display. The doors, windows, balconies, and roofs of the Adams House, as well as the private residences in the neighborhood, and the large stores and warehouses along Lake Street were crowded with ladies and other personsall cheering and welcoming the senator. At the depot, a procession consisting of the "Montgomery Guards," Capt. Gleason and the "Emmet Guards," andc., Lieut. Stuart commanding, acting as the military escort, was then formed. Judge Douglas was in an open barouche drawn by six horses, and was followed by the committee of arrangements in other carriages. The procession proceeded up Lake to Wabash Avenue, down Wabash Avenue to Dearborn street, and thence by Dearborn to the Tremont House.

Throughout the whole route of the procession, the senator was greeted from house top and window, from street, from awning post and balcony by every demonstration of grateful welcome.

THE SCENE AT THE TREMONT

As early as half past six o'clock people began to collect around the Tremont House. The omnibusses from Union Park, and from the southern and northern limits of the city, were crowded with suburban residents, and people came on foot from the remotest parts of the city, taking up eligible standing places around the hotel.

At about half past seven the booming of cannon on the lake shore having announced the arrival of the train, it was the signal for the assembling of thousands of others who rapidly filled up every vacant spot in Lake street, from State, for the distance of a block and a half. Dearborn street was also thronged from Lake to Randolph. The area occupied by the people, packed together in one dense mass, was considerably over fifty thousand square feet. In addition to this, every window and roof within hearing distance was occupied, a large portion of the occupants being ladies. The assemblage of people who welcomed in vociferous and prolonged shouts of joy the return of Senator Douglas numbered at the least calculation thirty thousand.

Chicago has never before witnessed such a sight. A field of human forms parted with difficulty as the procession passed through, and closed instantly behind it, with the surge and roar of the waters of a sea; an ocean of upturned faces, extending beyond the furthest limits to which the senator's powerful voice could reach, from which broke one spontaneous burst of applause as he appeared upon the balcony before them! Over all the light of the illumination, and the glare and glitter of the fireworks, spread an appearance which is indescribable!

The building just across the street fron the Tremont, on Lake, occupied by Jno. Parmly, hat manufacturer, and others, was finely illuminated, and a handsome transparency was displayed, bearing the words "Welcome to Stephen A. Douglas, the Defender of Popular Sovereignty."

.

THE SPEECHES

Chas. Walker, Esq., then appeared on the Lake Street balcony and in a very neat address, welcomed Senator Douglas to his constituents from a prolonged, but glorious struggle in which he defended and maintained the right.

Senator Douglas responded in a speech of over an hour in which he briefly reviewed the history of the past and the prospect of the future.

We could not but remember the scene of 1854, when instead of welcoming huzzas he was greeted with denunciation. The past, however, is gone; the present is upon us; and instead of the mere handful who indorsed his course in 1854, he now can count thousands who have approved his course, and an united constituency who applaud and admire the fidelity with which he has adhered to his principles and to the pledges he made to the people.

THE OVATION TO SENATOR DOUGLAS

The followers of Senator Douglas are straining their utmost powers to make the demonstration in behalf of their champion on his return home, a great and "glorious" affair, this evening. If it does not prove imposing, and if there is not a tremendous outward show of "enthusiasm" displayed on the occasion, it will not be for lack of effort on the part of the Senator's more active worshippers to render it so. They have been begging and scraping together all the spare dollars, shillings, dimes and six pences that could be obtained, for the last few weeks,have bought powder enough to supply the Utah warhave expended large sums in getting up banners and devicesand have laid out not a small sum in hiring men and boys to make up a big procession and make a big noise. Surely, after such extensive preparations, we have a right to anticipate a great time, and shall expect to see the lionized Senator perfectly emblazoned in the glory of triumphant honors.

Personal. Hon. A. Lincoln, 0. H. Browning, Judge I. O. Wilkinson of Rock Island, and other distinguished gentlemen from different parts of the State are at present in the city, in attendance on the U. S. District Court.

SPEECH OF SENATOR DOUGLAS LAST NIGHT

Several thousand people, amongst whom were many Republicans, who were present as a matter of curiosityassembled in front of the Tremont House last evening, on the occasion of the reception of

Senator Douglas, to hear what account he had to give of himself and what he had to say in reference to the political topics of the day.

He spoke for an hour and a half, in his usual styledispensing "soft-soap" quite freely, setting himself forth as a hero of no common order, and indulging even more than ordinarily in that inexorable habit of misrepresentation, and prevarication which appears in political matters to have become a sort of second nature to him.

Dropping the Kansas question, he next paid his respects to Mr. Lincoln and the speech that gentleman made at Springfield at the late Republican State Convention. He considered Mr. Lincoln a "kind, amiable, high-minded gentleman, a good citizen, and an honorable opponent," but took exception to the sentiments of his speech.

He repeated, almost word for word, the language of his last year's Springfield speech in regard to "negro equality" and very falsely imputed to Mr. Lincoln this doctrine of "negro equality," while the fact is that Mr. Lincoln has no more to do with negroes, or the question of placing negroes on an equality with white men, than Douglas has to do with the Americanizing of the Hottentots or the Fejee Islanders.

The following scene, as described by the Tribune, took place preliminary to the speech:

Shortly before eight o'clock the procession from the depot, preceded by a band of music, and two companies of militia, reached the corner of Lake and Dearborn streets, from Randolph. The hack drivers charged furiously on the dense throng and by dint of whipping and swearing, the carriage containing Mr. Douglas was brought up to the north entrance of the house. At this juncture a blockhead on the upper balcony commenced firing off rockets, and of course made a dozen horses crazy. Those attached to the carriage in which Mr. Douglas sat, plunged frantically in every direction. Several persons were bruised. One man had his leg broken in three places, and was borne fainting into a drug store. Mr. Douglas escaped indoors, and almost immediately reappeared on the north balcony, when Charles Walker, Esq., commenced his reception speech.

At this point of the proceedings a furious battle commenced in the street between the crowd and the remaining hack drivers, who persisted insanely in plowing through the living sea in front of the building. In the confusion and excitement, Mr. Walker's speech came to an abrupt and embarrassing terminationleaving people uncertain whether he had forgotten the balance, or had adopted the novel and peculiar way of welcoming a Senator. Not one man in fifty of the entire audience knew that he had made a speech at all. The battle in the street below was kept up for some ten minutes with various results,one man being knocked down with the butt end of a whip, and a driver being pulled off his seat three times in five minutes. The horses were finally extricated and Mr. Douglas commenced.

THE DIFFERENCES

Four years ago Senator Douglas returned to Chicago from Washington and attempted to speak to the people in justification of his course in the United States Senate, but was denied a hearing. And, indeed, as most of our readers will recollect, when he did make the effort he was assailed and driven from the platform. The Chicago people would not listen to him; nor did they permit him the right of speech at all, so incensed were they against him for his support of the Kansas-Nebraska bill.

Four years have elapsed since then and the city which hunted, denounced and assailed the "little giant," makes the occasion of his arrival a source of public rejoicing. In another place we have alluded to his triumphant entry into the city on last Friday. Indeed, it is conceded that for magnificence and unanimity it excelled any demonstration of the kind ever witnessed west of the Allegheny Mountains.

RECEPTION AND SPEECH OF SENATOR DOUGLAS

Chicago, July 9, 11 p. m.

Senator Douglas was received here this evening, with great display. At one o'clock, a committee of four hundred persons of Chicago and the adjoining counties, proceeded to Michigan City, where they met the train, and escorted Mr. Douglas to this city, and, on his arrival, he was greeted with vociferous cheering from the people, and the firing of cannon. A procession was immediately formed, and Mr. Douglas was conducted to the Tremont House, where he was welcomed in a brief speech in behalf of the citizens, by Charles Walker, President of the Board of Trade.
Mr. Lincoln was present and heard Mr. Douglas. Fireworks were discharged in several parts of the city. The number of persons in attendance is variously estimated at from fifteen to twenty-five thousand.
At the Douglas meeting, Lincoln was accorded the courtesy of "a good seat," as he said, and, according to his custom four years before in the senatorial campaign, he arose the following evening at the same place to reply to Douglas. Quite naturally, the Chicago newspapers varied in their report of the meeting, according to their political complexions.

SPEECH OF HON. ABRAHAM LINCOLN IN REPLY TO SENATOR DOUGLAS

Enthusiastic Reception of Mr. Lincoln by the Republicans of Chicago

The audience assembled to hear Hon. Abraham Lincoln on Saturday evening was in point of numbers, about three-fourths as large as that of the previous evening, when Douglas held forth; and in point of enthusiasm, about four times as great. The crowd extended from the corner of Lake and Dearborn Streets the whole length of the Tremont House, and as on the evening previous, the balconies, windows and roofs of the adjoining buildings were filled with attentive spectatorsladies and gentlemen. The only advertisement of the meeting consisted of a notice in the Saturday morning papers, and a few handbills distributed during the day. The essential difference in the two demonstrations was simply that the Lincoln audience was enthusiastically for Lincoln, and the Douglas was but qualified in favor of anybody. This will be admitted by any fair-minded man who witnessed both demonstrations. The Douglas authorities estimated the crowd of Friday evening at 30,000or something more than the whole male adult population of the city. We presume that 12,000 is a liberal reckoning for that evening, and that 9,000 would about cover the gathering of Saturday night.

During the progress of Mr. Lincoln's speech a procession of four hundred men from the Seventh ward including the German Republican Club, arrived on the ground, preceded by a band of music, and carrying the Seventh ward banner. They were received with loud and continued cheers from the audience.

Mr. Lincoln was introduced by C. L. Wilson, Esq., and as he made his appearance he was greeted with a perfect storm of applause. For some moments the enthusiasm continued unabated. At last, when by a wave of his hand partial silence was restored, Mr. Lincoln spoke.

THE MEETING SATURDAY NIGHT

At an early hour Saturday evening, the street in front of the Tremont House began to be filled with an eager crowd. A band of music discoursed from the balcony of the Tremont, and rockets blazed in different directions until about 8+1/2 o'clock, the gathering in the meantime having been swelled to thousands, presenting literally a sea of faces.

Shortly afterward Mr. Lincoln appeared on the balcony, and was greeted with a perfect storm of cheers.

The feature of the evening, was the arrival of the German Republican Club of the Seventh Ward, with a band of music, and their new banner. They were vociferously greeted with the wildest kind of hurrahs.

Mr. Lincoln devoted himself to replying to the speech of Senator Douglas, and considering the brief time he had for preparation, it must be conceded that he did it effectually.

From the Chicago Union

LINCOLN ON THE STUMP

Burlesque on the Doug-las Ovation

Yesterday (Saturday) placards appeared on the streets; and a band went round in a wagon to announce to the Republicans that Hon. Abraham Lincoln would reply to Hon. S. A. Douglas from the Tremont House balcony.Rockets were fired to show the spot where Lincoln would talk, and at 8+1/2 o'clock, not less than 3,000 persons of all parties had assembled. The lamps marked with the names of States, which had been set up for Douglas, were re-lit; but it was remarkable that those of the slave States burned very badly, and some one from the crowd suggested that a black republican meeting could do with seventeen lamps. Bye-and-Bye Bross came forward and stood between two lamps, the light playing on his generous countenance, when there arose a shout of "Bross," "Lincoln." A stentorian voice cried, "Fellows, Bross will do as well," when there arose a shout of Bross, amidst which the worthy Deacon retired, blushing. He remarked,

when behind (Bross is his own Boswell,) "They got their eyes on me, did they not?" Band of music plays.Then there were cries of Long John, Little John, George Brown, Smart, etc. After a disagreeable wait, C. L. Wilson, Esq., of the Journal, introduced Mr. Lincoln. Bross went forward and called for cheers, when the crowd cried out "Lincoln, stand where Bross is," and he did. We shall not attempt to give Mr. Lincoln's speech. It was a rambling affair. Mr. L. thought he was mentioned in such a way that he could not refuse to reply to him. He commenced to read from the Senator's speech.
He argued against the allegation of Judge Douglas that an alliance existed between the Republicans and the National Democrats. He denied it.

Douglas is not a live lion but a Russian rugged bear. He objected to being slain. Let him remember the allies took Sebastopol. He confessed he rather liked the disaffection of the Buchanan Democracy, because it would divide the party. But he had never paid to them. He wanted to know what had become of squatter sovereignty. He would read them something from Douglas. He thought Douglas did right in opposing Lecompton, because all the Republicans voted with him. He did not leave them to vote against it. Who defeated Lecomptonwas it Judge Douglas! He furnished three votes, and the Black Republicans twenty against it. Now, who did it. He'd put the proposition in a different way. The Republican party would have defeated Lecompton without Douglas. He reiterated his views upon the matter of the ultimate extinction of slavery. The speaker attempted a reply to Democratic principles, amid some applause, and some spicy interruptions. We left when Deacon Bross announced that the Seventh Ward are coming. Band played, Hocklets fizzled, and we mizzled.

LINCOLN'S REPLY TO DOUGLAS

"We today occupy considerable of our space with the speech of Hon. Abraham Lincoln, in reply to Senator Douglas' speech of Friday evening..... The war has begun. The first fire has been exchanged by the two contestants. Those who will read the speech we publish today, will perceive that the Little Giant is already wounded in several vital parts. In sound, manly argument, Lincoln is too much for him. While the former shakes his black locks vain-gioriously and explodes in mere fustian of sound and smoke, the latter quietly unassumingly but effectually drives home argument after argument, heavy as cannon balls, and sharp as two-edged swords, until his adversary is so thoroughly riddled, cut up and "used up," that in the view of discriminating men, nothing remains of him but a ghostly appearance.

SENATOR DOUGLAS IN CHICAGO

We devote much space in our news colums to the reproduction of reports in the Chicago papers of the reception of Senator Douglas in that city Friday last, and his speech on that occasion. His competitor, Hon. Abram Lincoln, sat near him, marked attentively all he said, and replied to him from the same place the following evening. We have not yet a report of Mr. Lincoln's remarks. The speech of Douglas was able and bold, and it appears from some things said of Lincoln, that his personal relations with that gentleman are friendly.The indications are that the political campaign in Illinois will be quite exciting and the contest close, and that Douglas will succeed in being re-elected to the U. S. Senate.

The debate in Illinois, between Lincoln and Douglas, is the ablest and the most important that has ever taken place in any of the States, on the great question which has so long agitated the country, elected and defeated Presidential candidates, built up and broken down parties. It is the opening of the question for 1860. There the real battle has begun, by broadsides too, from the heaviest artillery. Douglas is matchless in debate, and stands upon the only national platform. Lincoln is able, and does full justice to the bad cause he

advocates. He is the champion of anti-slavery in the North. It is the one idea that has brought him forward as the candidate of his party.....

PRESIDENTIAL CANDIDATES

As to the Southern Democratic candidates, the leading men are Senator Hunter and Gov. Wise of Virginia, the former representing Administration, the latter anti-Administration views on the Kansas question. Senator Slidell, of Louisiana, Secretary Floyd, of Virginia, and Hon. Alexander H. Stephens, of Georgia, are also spoken of.

The Times postpones the chances of Senator Douglas indefinitely, on account of his quarrel with the administration, and the fact that he is from a Northern State, two circumstances which render his nomination entirely out of the question.

Among the Republican candidates, the Times places the name of Col. Fremont first on the list; next Mr. Seward, followed by Mr. Crittenden, Gov. Banks, of Mass., Gov. Chase, of Ohio, and Judge McLean.

From its beginning the Illinois campaign attracted widespread attention. It meant more than state issues and state results. The fate of "squatter sovereignty," the triumph or defeat of the administration, the presidential nominations to be made in the next national conventions, indeed, the future of the Union was felt to depend in no small degree upon the outcome of these debates. Eastern newspapers at once dispatched special reporters to the scene and they outlined the situation for their readers.

POLITICS IN ILLINOIS

Chicago, Ill., August 13, 1858

The interest in politics increases here as the campaign progresses. Illinois is regarded as the battle-ground of the year, and the results of this contest are held to be of the highest importance to the wellfare of the country and the success of the great contending parties. The Republican Convention of June 16, after placing a state ticket in nomination, named as its choice for United States senator to succeed Mr. Douglas, Mr. Lincoln, of Springfield. This expression met at once the approval of the Republicans of the state. Mr. Lincoln was regarded as the man for the place. A native of Kentucky, where he belonged to the class of "poor whites," he came early to Illinois. Poor unfriended, uneducated, a day-laborer, he has distanced all these disadvantages, and in the profession of the law he has risen steadily to a competence, and to the position of an intelligent, shrewd and well balanced man. Familiarly known as "Long Abe," he is a popular speaker, and a cautious, thoughtful politician, capable of taking a high position as a statesman and legislator. His nomination was proof that the Republicans of Illinois were determined in their hostility to Mr. Douglas, and that no latter-day conversion of his, however luminous it might appear to some eastern eyes, could blind them to the fact that in him were embodied the false and fatal principles against which they were organized. They had grown mighty in their opposition to Douglas, and in his defeat they were certain of an enlarged and a well-established party. Even Mr. Douglas's anti-Lecomptonism could not excuse or palliate his past errors; nor did it incline them in the least degree to sympathize with him. Save in this one respect, he was, as ever, the firm upholder of Dred Scottism, and the constant apologist and defender of the Federal Administration and the measures which it urged upon an unwilling country. The people of Illinois felt certain that they knew best the sentiment of their state, and they repudiated the counsels of those who suggested that Douglas was a good-enough Republican, and that he might be used to break down the democratic party here and in the northwest. The present attitude of Mr. Douglas, so entirely consistent with his antecedents, is good evidence that the Republicans in Illinois did well to contemn the time-serving and dangerous suggestions that emanated from Washington and New York, and which had voice in many influential journals at the East. Mr. Douglas, in all his speeches, claims to be a democrat, and demands the support of democrats in his assault upon Republicanism. The "Little Giant" is unchanged in no respect; and as the canvass grows warmer, the breech widens, and his actual position becomes more clearly defined.

He is of other material, altogether, than that which makes Republicanism. He is still an out-and-out pro-slavery man. In one of his recent speeches he stopped to read the dispatch announcing Blair's defeat in St. Louis, as the overthrow of "negro equality" and all that sort of stuff that forms the staple of democratic rhetoric.

It is a foregone conclusion, therefore, that under no circumstances can the Republicans of Illinois show any favor to Mr. Douglas. In fighting him, they fight democracy in one of its worst forms. It seems to be equally a conclusion that the administration democrats of Illinois are utterly hostile to Douglas. The democratic split, while widening every day, is as marked and bitter as in the battle of the Shells. "Danite" and Douglasite are names of hostility as deep as that once existing between Hard and Soft. Perhaps another truce at Charleston, as hollow as that at Cincinnati, may be needed to "harmonize" things. Senator Slidell has been here to look on, perhaps to "fix" matters. Stephens of Georgia is here now, ostensibly to have his portrait painted by Healy, but really to see what can be done to adjust these difficulties. The prospect is reported to be not flattering. The Buchanan men propose to carry their anti-Douglas feeling even to the least important county nominations. The democracy must choose whom they will serve, and come out flat-footed for the Post-office, or for the Douglas exegesis of popular sovereignty.

Douglas is working like a lion. He is stumping the state, everywhere present, and everywhere appealing to his old lieges to stand by him. Never did feudal baron fight more desperately against the common superior of himself and his retainers. In the Egypt of Southern Illinois the senator has been always strong, but the ties that bound him to the Egyptians are melting before the incessant charges that he is no democrat. That cry is fatal to the faith of many of his once most reliable friends. Democracy must be done, though Douglas falls.

Lincoln, too, is actively engaged. His senatorial nomination has sent him to the field, and he is working with an energy and zeal which counterbalance the spirit and dogged resolution of his opponent. Lincoln is battling for the right, and Douglas is desperately struggling to save himself from utter political ruin. He is losing strength daily, while Lincoln is surely gaining upon him. You will observe as a new feature, even in western politics, that Mr. Lincoln has a State Convention nomination for the Senate, and that he is stumping the state for his party, while the legislature to be elected is to have the responsibility of electing the senator. But with this endorsement, no Republican member of the state legislature would dare to bolt the significant expression of the Springfield Convention. Mr. Douglas, on the other hand, has no nomination. Returning home, he found Mr. Lincoln prepared, and at once he mounted the platform and opened upon him. He is stumping for himself, and trying to vindicate his course to the people at large on the one hand, and to the administration scoffers on the other.

.

SENATORIAL CONTEST IN ILLINOIS

The Republican candidate for United States Senator, the Hon. Abraham Lincoln, was present on Saturday evening when Mr. Douglas made his address published in Tuesday's Times to the crowd assembled in honor of his arrival in Chicago. On Monday evening Mr. Lincoln replied to his distinguished competitor, and we give his speech in full this morning. He, too, received an enthusiastic welcome and the war between the two champions was fitly inaugurated in the chief city of Illinois..... Until November, therefore, the contest will go on with increasing vigor. Mr Douglas has an undertaking on hand which will task his utmost powers, and he is not the man to flinch from a contest because the odds are against him.

RECEPTION OF LINCOLN

On Monday night there was a large gathering in the legislative hall of the Capitol to hear the Honorable Abraham Lincoln in reply to Mr. Douglas. Mr. Lincoln, though not perhaps so well calculated for a leader as Senator Douglas, is a remarkably able man. In addition to his talents as a lawyer, he has many personal qualities which have endeared him to the people of Illinois, and will be beyond all question the strongest opponent that could be found in the State to oppose Mr. Douglas.

It is, we believe somewhat of an anomaly for a Senator of the United States to be stumping the State, and another who wishes to be Senator following in his wake, yet thus it is at the present time in Illinois, and none can have heard either these gentlemen speak without being impressed and highly gratified with the fact that whenever reference is made by either to the other, it is in the kindest, most

courteous and dignified manner. The approaching political contest between Senator Douglas and Mr. Lincoln will be one of the severest we have had in the State, but that it will result in the reelection of Douglas there appears to be at present very little doubt.

The admirable and thoroughly Republican speech of Mr. Lincoln in reply to Judge Douglas, published in our last, seemed to require no comment; yet a single remark with reference to the origin and attitude of the rival canvassers may not be out of place. Judge Douglas, who regards Slavery as an affair of climate and latitude, is a native of Free Vermont; Mr. Lincoln, who esteems Slavery a National evil, and hopes that our Union may one day be all Free, was born and reared in slave-holding Kentucky. These gentlemen would seem respectively to have "conquered their prejudices" founded in early impressions. We shall watch with interest the progress of their canvass.

SENATOR DOUGLAS

Senator Douglas, little giant though he be, can hardly fail to suffer somewhat from the wear and tear of the life he leads..... The adjournment of Congress brings no peace to the Senator from Illinois Strong as he was in that state,holding as he thought he did, the democratic party at home in his handhe finds that he has lost ground there. The Administration has been at work with all the power which its patronage and influence gives it to prevent the re-election of Mr. Douglas to the Senate. And he is obliged to go to work again, this time with his coat off, stumping the State and addressing the people, with the thermometer ranging somewhere between 96 and 100 in the shade. And not only this, while the democracy are very forgetful of their old comrade and ungrateful for the services he has so frequently done them in past years, the republicans, generally speaking have not a particle of faith in Mr. Douglas' professions. He has not their confidence and is plainly unable to win them to his support. Mr. Lincoln, the republican candidate, follows him wherever he addresses the people, and has the best of the argument.... As it is, he lost his temper and in reply to some remarks of Mr. Trumbull made at a public meeting at Chicago, indulged in language which he will probably be ashamed to read in print.

The favorable manner in which Douglas' speech was received by the Democrats in the city of Chicago was a disappointment to the supporters of Buchanan in his contest with Douglas and immediate steps were taken to curb the latter's popularity in Illinois. The administration machinery was put in motion and, before many days had passed, lists of proscribed postmasters and of other federal employees favorable to Douglas began to appear in the newspapers. The Union, the administration organ in Washington, devoted columns of space to show why the Democrats of Illinois should not support Douglas, and urged them to vote for Judge

Breese, who was faint-heartedly put forward in opposition to the Little Giant. Senator Trumbull, bound to support Lincoln because of his sacrifice four years before, as well as by party ties and natural hostility toward Douglas, took the stump in a series of abusive attacks on Douglas, which drew from the latter equally caustic and offensive rejoinders. Without a formal nomination or indorsement by the people of Illinois, ridiculed as a "my-party" candidate, and facing the loss of the federal patronage, Douglas entered upon the greatest of his many battles for supremacya contest surpassing that waged two years later for the presidency, when he was in a hopeless situation from the beginning of the campaign. Alone and unaided, he faced in the lists Trumbull and Lincoln, the best debaters afforded by the Republicans in the West, and probably equaled only by Seward in the East.

DOUGLAS TO TAKE THE STUMP

Judge Douglas has left the Democratic party, or the party has left him. He opposed the Administration in its darling measure to enslave Kansasand there is no forgiveness for him. He sees that his fate is sealed; but he is determined to die hard. Before he retires from the field, a defeated and disappointed man, he will give the "Nationals" such stabs as will forever finish the party in this State. He has already turned State's evidence against themas the greatest rogues always doand show up their rascalities. We shall have more of it this fall; and we would advise the Buchaneers to be prepared for a skinning.

SENATOR DOUGLAS

His campaign through this state will pretty effectually destroy the hopes of the Repubhcan party; and Abe Lincoln, who compared himself to a "living dog" and Douglas to a "dead lion" will rapidly discover that instead of "living" he is one of the smallest of defunct puppies. He measures strength with Douglas! His comparison in some degrees was trueit is very much like a puppy-dog fighting a lion.Pittsfield Democrat.

THE CANVASS IN ILLINOIS

Illinois is just now the theatre of the most momentous political contest, whether we consider the eminence of the contestants or the consequences which may result from it, that has occured in this country in any state canvass since the defeat of Silas Wright for Governor in 1846. Nor are the contestants dissimilar. Both were regarded by their friends as material from which Presidents should be made; both were victims of treachery at Washington, and both were betrayed for venturing to propose a limit to the exactions of the nullifiers and disunionists......

One week after his triumphant reception at Chicago, Douglas began a tour of the state which was to continue during the four summer months. He made elaborate preparations for the beginning of the journey, traveling in a special train of coaches which included a flat car upon which was mounted a small cannon. The opposition press did not fail to ridicule the novel method of firing salutes as the train drew near a station instead of running the risk of not receiving a welcoming salute from the inhabitants of the city being approached. "Douglas' powder" suffered a run of pleasantries; kegs of powder tagged for Douglas were reported seen at various stations; and Republican papers circulated the story that Douglas was obliged to mortgage his Chicago home and even then to solicit funds in New York to carry on the expensive campaign. On the other hand, the Democratic press praised his action in transferring to the new University of Chicago the ground on which its buildings stood as the deed of a noble man of means. The first important stop made by the special train was at Bloomington.

DOUGLAS AT BLOOMINGTON

Hon. Stephen A. Douglas arrived in this city at half past three o'clock yesterday afternoon. The train on which he arrived was tastefully decorated with flags and on each side of the baggage car were the words "S. A. Douglas, the Champion of Popular Sovereignty." About a thousand personsmore than one half of whom were Republicanswitnessed Judge D's arrival. Just before the cars reached the depot Pullen's Brass Band commenced playing "Hail Columbia" and when the cars stopped, the Bloomington Guards commenced firing a national salute of thirty-two guns. Judge Douglas was in the hindmost passenger caran open car, upon which was placed a brass sixpounder, bringing up the rear.

At seven o'clock in the evening the Court House bell rang and Judge Douglas escorted by the Guards, the Brass Band and a goodly number of Democrats, proceeded to the public square. He was welcomed by Dr. Roe, who spoke for about five minutes and concluded by introducing Judge Douglas.

The Judge commenced speaking at half past seven, and concluded at a quarter before ten. His speech did not differ materially from the one made by him in Chicago on the evening of the ninth.

He spoke to an audience of about two thousand persons. His Democratic listeners were highly pleased with his speech. They viewed it as a masterly effort and we are willing to admit that the Judge did, on the whole, make a very good speech in a very bad cause.

As soon as Judge Douglas retired, loud calls were made for Hon. Abraham Lincoln. Mr. Lincoln held back for a little while, but the crowd finally succeeded in inducing him to come upon the stand. He was received with three rousing cheers much louder than those given to Judge Douglas. He remarked that he appeared before the audience for the purpose of saying that he would take an early opportunity to give his views to the citizens of this place regarding the matters spoken of in Judge Douglas' speech."This meeting," said Mr. Lincoln, "was called by the friends of Judge Douglas, and it would be improper for me to address it." Mr. Lincoln then retired amid loud cheering.

Leaving Bloomington, the senatorial train proceeded to the real objective pointSpringfield, the state capital, the home of Lincoln, and a stronghold of Douglas supporters. Here the senator addressed an enormous gathering of people in a grove adjacent to the city. He explained his objections to the Lecompton constitution, asserting that it did not represent the free will of the whole people of Kansas, although he did not object to its pro-slavery tendency. Turning his attention to Lincoln, he pronounced his attitude toward the non-extension of slavery as virtually a war upon that institution and ridiculed his proposition to get a new law from Congress which would undo the Dred Scott decision. He bore especially hard on Lincoln's defense of the black man and charged that he desired black and white to be social equals.

SENATOR DOUGLAS AT THE CAPITAL

WILLIAMSVILLE

Here the train with Senator Douglas was met,the rain pouring down in torrents the while. The cannon thundered welcome for welcomethe shouts of the passengers joined m swelling the uproarious greeting; the several bands struck up stirring airs, and amid the storm, of rain, shouts, guns and music, the trains were joined and sped southward. When within two miles of Springfield the cannon, at minute intervals, announced the coming of our great guest. At precisely three o'clock the train arrived.

AT SPRINGFIELD

According to the arrangements the train stopped beside the beautiful grove of Mr. Edwards, on the northern boundary of the city, where, notwithstanding the previous drenching rain, thousands of people were awaiting the arrival of the distinguished visitor. The cannon on the cars boomed in response to cannon on the grounds, barely equalled in their thunders by the hurras of the crowd. The grove was gaily decorated with national flags, with significant mottoes, the whole forming a scene which filled the heart of every democrat present with prideConspicuous among these banners we will note was one very large pennant, with "Douglas," in broad letters upon its folds, got up by the Springfield employees of the work shops of the Chicago and St. Louis Road. Upon the stoppage of the train the committee of reception, preceded by the "Capital Guards" and the capital band, escorted Mr. Douglas to the stand, where Mr. B. S. Edwards welcomed him in a neat address, which welcome was reiterated by the hearty cheers of the large assemblage which he represented. To this Senator

Douglas responded. We give both the address and reply in today's paper.
Senator Douglas' speech was received as it justly deserved, the reader will admit. Cheer upon cheer responded to his many happy points and forcible argumentation.
The crowd upon the ground numbered between five and six thouand. The drenching rain which immediately preceded the arrival of the train, and which made the grounds muddy and uncomfortable, kept away as many more, who were present in the city to participate in the reception. Especially is it to be regretted, that the committee's arrangements for the accommodation of the ladies were rendered unavailable on account of the rain, but notwithstanding, there were hundreds of them present in carriages, and many on foot, in mud joining in the cheering welcome to our distinguished guest. The counties immediately around us furnished large delegations,

and hundreds were here from remote parts of the state. From the south a train of twelve cars were filled with people from Madison, Macoupin, Jersey, Greene, Montgomery, St. Claire, Monroe and other countiesone of these cars bearing a conspicuous pledge, in bold lettering"Madison for Douglas!"Another, "Jersey all right for Douglas!"with a sixpounder on a platform car in the rear, this train came thundering into town at noon.
From the east a train, decorated with national banners, bearing delegations from the counties along the line of the G. W. Road, Macon, Piatt, Champaign, andc., arrived at 12, and simultaneously, from the west, another train of ten cars, with delegations from Morgan, Scott, and Pike, covered with the stars and stripes, and a cannon to tell their coming, arrived.
From our own county, notwithstanding the busy time of our farmers, and the rainy day, the people poured into town from all directionsThe town was alive with the masses, who wanted to see and to welcome Douglas. From the state house flag-staff streamed the national flag across the streets around the square hung immense banners, many of the buildings fronting the square were tastefully ornamented with flags, interspersed with mottoes, all speaking the one idea"welcome to Douglas."

SPEECH OF SENATOR DOUGLAS

Mr. Edwards having introduced Senator Douglas to the audience, Senator Douglas said:

"I will not recur to the scenes which took place all over this country in 1854 when that Nebraska bill passed. I could then travel from Boston to Chicago by the light of my own effigies, in consequence of having stood up for it. I leave it to you to say how I met that storm, and whether I quailed under it: whether I did not 'face the music,' justify the principle and pledge my life to carry it out."....

Meanwhile Lincoln had returned to Springfield and although he was not present at the Douglas meeting in the afternoon, he took advantage of the presence of many strangers in the city to address the people at a public meeting at the State House in the evening. He devoted the speech largely to repelling the charges made by Douglas against him of disunion sentiment, forcible resistance to the Dred Scott decision, and a desire for negro equality. He also renewed his charge that the Dred Scott decision was a conspiracy to which Douglas was a party Douglas was not present at the meeting, having already departed on his tour of the state. In this irregular manner began a campaign, which was speedily turned into a series of formal debates through a challenge sent by Lincoln to Douglas.

CHAPTER III. THE CHALLENGE

After conferring with the Democratic Committee at Springfield, Douglas gave out a list of his appointments covering July and a large part of August, ending with Ottawa, August 21. Lincoln's friends also prepared a list of Republican meetings, in some cases coinciding with the Democratic dates but generally following them a day later. In his Springfield speech, Lincoln distinctly stated that he was not present when Douglas made his speech in the grove during the afternoon and had no intention of making his remarks a reply. The previous day at Bloomington he refused to heed the calls of the crowd for a reply at the close of a Douglas meeting. Nevertheless, soon after the appointed meetings began, the Douglas papers made complaint that Lincoln was transgressing the ethics of campaigning by following their candidate and taking advantage of his crowds.

The Chicago Times launches out into a personal attack upon Mr. Lincoln for presuming to be present when Mr. Douglas speaks. One would think from this that Mr. Douglas has a patent right to audiences in Illinois. We hope that Mr. Lincoln will continue to follow up Senator Douglas with a sharp stick, even if it does make his organ howl with rage.

Geneseo, Ill., August 15, 1858

Douglas and Lincoln are stumping the state and a right merry time they have of it; wherever the Little Giant happens to be, Abe is sure to turn up and be a thorn in his side.

X.

AN AUDIENCE WANTED

It was Japhet, we believe, whose adventures in search of his father, furnished the novelist with the plot of a popular romance. There are but few of our readers who have not known, or at least heard of physicians unable, even in the midst of sickness, to obtain patients, lawyers unable to obtain clients, and actors unable to draw houses. But we venture to say that never before was there heard of in any political canvass in Illinois, of a candidate unable to obtain an audience to hear him! But such is the fact. Abe Lincoln, the candidate of all the Republicans, wants an audience. He came up to Chicago, and, taking advantage of the enthusiasm of Douglas' reception, made a speech here; he went to Bloomington, and, at the Douglas meeting, advertised himself for a future occasion; at Springfield he distributed handbills at the Douglas meeting imploring the people to hear him. The Springfield attempt was a failure. He came to Chicago, and declared it impossible for him to get the people to turn out to hear him, and then it was resolved to try and get him a chance to speak to the crowds drawn out to meet and welcome Douglas. That proposition was partially declined and another substituted; but yet the cringing, crawling creature is hanging at the outskirts of Douglas' meetings, begging the people to come and hear him. At Clinton he rose up at the Democratic meeting, and announced his intention to speak at night, but only 250 persons could be induced to attend his meeting.

He went yesterday to Monticello in Douglas' train; poor, desperate creature, he wants an audience; poor unhappy mortal, the people won't turn out to hear him, and he must do something, even if that something is mean, sneaking and disreputable!

We have a suggestion to make to Mr. Juddthe next friend of Lincoln. There are two very good circuses and menageries traveling through the State;

these exhibitions always draw good crowds at country towns. Mr. Judd, in behalf of his candidate, at a reasonable expense, might make arrangements with the managers of these exhibitions to include a speech from Lincoln in their performances. In this way Lincoln could get good audiences, and his friends be relieved from the mortification they all feel at his present humiliating position.

DOUGLAS AND LINCOLN

The Times growls because Mr. Lincoln made a speech at Clinton, at night, in reply to that of Senator Douglas, delivered in the afternoon, and that he "went to Monticello in Douglas' train".

We suppose Douglas owns neither the railroad trains he travels on, nor the people whom he addresses. We hope Mr. Lincoln will answer Senator Douglas at every point. If he will not invite him to address the same audiences, Lincoln will have the "closing argument" to meetings of his own. According to authority quoted in the Senator's Springfield speech, "there is no law against it."
Lincoln, unable to gather a crowd himself, follows up Douglas and attempts to reply ; but they are mere attempts. His hearers soon become satisfied and by the time he is done begging for a seat in the Senate he finds himself minus an audience.

WHO FURNISHES THE AUDIENCES

Under this caption the Chicago Press and Tribune, of the 23d inst., proceeds to argue that at the joint discussions between Douglas and Lincoln thus far, the friends of the latter have been largely in the ascendanthence Mr. Lincoln draws the greatest crowds. This conclusion is characteristic of the logical proclivities of that paper, and only lacks one featuretruth.

If this assertion is true, why then does Mr. Lincoln persist in following up Judge Douglas for the ostensible purpose of taking advantage of the large audiences assembled to hear him? For instance look at his last demonstration at Sullivan, where, through his uncourteous behavior, a riot was almost precipitated.

The fact is, Mr. Lincoln can't draw large crowdsthe sympathy of the people is not with himconsequently he resorts to this highly disreputable course to make a show. The Chicago organ cannot palm off such logic upon the people of Illinois.

DOUGLAS AND LINCOLN ON THE STUMP

The Chicago Times states that Douglas and Lincoln met on the 27 ult. at Clinton. The former spoke for three hours, and the latter replied at an evening meeting. The Times indulges in a tirade against Mr. Lincoln, an extract from which will serve to indicate the bitterness of feeling that enters into this contest:

Lincoln was present during the delivery of the speech, sitting immediately in front of Senator Douglas, but rendered invisible from the stand by a gentleman in green goggles, whom he used as a shield and cover. After Senator Douglas had concluded, and the cheers which greeted him ceased, green goggles rose and proposed three cheers for Lincoln, which were given by about ten men who stood immediately around him. Mr. Lincoln then gradually lengthened out his long, lank proportions until he stood upon his feet, and with a desperate attempt at looking pleasant, said that he would not take advantage of Judge Douglas' crowd, but would address "sich" as liked to hear him in the evening at the Court House. Having made this announcement in a tone and with an air of a perfect "Uriah Heep," pleading his humility, and asking for forgiveness of Heaven for his enemies, he stood washing his hands with invisible soap in imperceptible water, until his friends, seeing that his mind was wandering, took him in charge, and bundled him off the ground......

Mr. Lincoln's course in following Senator Douglas is condemned here even by his friends. He explains it by saying that he challenged Judge Douglas to meet the people and address them together, which challenge had not been accepted. The unfairness and untruth of this statement made in Chicago you who have seen the correspondence know.

Douglas was devoting a large share of attention in these speeches to his fellow-senator, Trumbull, who had charged Douglas with a corrupt bargain in espousing the repeal of the Missouri Compromise measure. Strong language was used by each and rumors of a personal encounter likely to follow between the two men were common. Trumbull's speeches were widely quoted in the eastern press as "representative Republican doctrines." The Boston Daily Traveler headed its campaign letter, "Illinois, Trumbull and Douglas." Lincoln saw that he was likely to be ignored if Trumbull were permitted to monopolize the attention of Douglas and in that case his political chances would be jeopardized. Manifestly his only course was to challenge Douglas to a series of set debates in which the political issues of the day would replace the personal matters at stake between Douglas and Trumbull. After consulting with representative Republicans of the State, Lincoln sent the following letter to Douglas:

Chicago, Ill., July 24, 1858

Hon. S. A. Douglas.
My dear Sir: Will it be agreeable to you to make an arrangement for you and myself to divide time, and address the same audiences the present canvass? Mr. Judd, who will hand you this, is authorized to receive your answer; and, if agreeable to you, to enter into the terms of such agreement. Your obedient servant,
A. Lincoln

The same day Douglas replied to Lincoln:
Chicago, July 24, 1858

Hon. A. Lincoln.
Dear Sir: Your note of this date, in which you inquire if it would be agreeable to me to make an arrangement to divide the time and address the same audiences during the present canvass, was handed to me by Mr. Judd. Recent events have interposed difficulties in the way of such an arrangement.
I went to Springfield last week for the purpose of conferring with the Democratic State Central Committee upon the mode of conducting the canvass, and with them, and under their advice, made a list of appointments covering the entire period until late in October. The people of the several localities have been notified of the times and places of the meetings. Those appointments have all been made for Democratic meetings, and arrangements have been made by which the Democratic candidates for Congress, for the Legislature, and other offices, will be present and address the people. It is evident, therefore, that these various candidates, in connection with myself, will occupy the whole time of the day and evening, and leave no opportunity for other speeches.

Besides, there is another consideration which should be kept in mind. It has been suggested recently that an arrangement had been made to bring out a third candidate for the United States Senate, who, with yourself, should canvass the State in opposition to me, with no other purpose than to insure my defeat, by dividing the Democratic party for your benefit. If I should make this arrangement with you, it is more than probable that this other candidate, who has a common object with you, would desire to become a party to it, and claim the right to speak from the same stand; so that he and you, in concert, might be able to take the opening and closing speech in every case.

I cannot refrain from expressing my surprise, if it was your original intention to invite such an arrangement, that you should have waited until after I had made my appointments, inasmuch as we were both here in Chicago together for several days after my arrival, and again at Bloomington, Atlanta, Lincoln, and Springfield, where it was well known I went for the purpose of consulting with State Central Committee, and agreeing upon the plan of the campaign.

While, under these circumstances, I do not feel at liberty to make any arrangement which would deprive the Democratic candidates for Congress, State offices, and the Legislature, from participating in the discussion at the various meetings designated by the Democratic State Central Committee, I will, in order to accommodate you as far as it is in my power to do so, take the responsibility of making an arrangement with you for a discussion between us at one prominent point in each Congressional District in the State, except the second and sixth districts, where we have both spoken, and in each of which cases you had the concluding speech. If agreeable to you, I will indicate the following places as those most suitable in the several Congressional Districts at which we should speak, to wit: Freeport, Ottawa, Galesburg, Quincy, Alton, Jonesboro, and Charleston. I will confer with you at the earliest convenient opportunity in regard to the mode of conducting the debate, the times of meeting at the several places, subject to the condition that where appointments have already been made by the Democratic State Central Committee at any of those places, I must insist upon you meeting me at the times specified.

Very respectfully, your most obedient servant,

S. A. Douglas

This correspondence was at once given to the press and excited a variety of comment.

ABRAHAM LINCOLN

LINCOLN'S CHALLENGE TO DOUGLAS

Below will be found the challenge of Mr. Lincoln to Mr. Douglas, and the reply of the latter.

We do not think it argues very well for the courage of the Senator that he evades the challenge in the manner he does, nor much for his courtesy when asked to confer with the Chairman of the Republican State Central Committee in regard to the times and places, that he should himself proceed to designate seven places where Mr. Lincoln must meet him, if at all.

The friends of Senator Douglas claim that Mr. Lincoln is no match for him, before the people. Every canvass for the last twenty years has found these two champions of their respective parties side by side with each other, and often addressing the same audience, and Mr. Lincoln never asked any favor of his adversary. He does not now. If Mr. Douglas really felt his superiority, those who know him will be slow to believe that he would not take advantage of it. He, however, shows the white feather, and, like a trembling Felix skulks behind the appointments of the emasculate Democratic State Central Committee!

The challenge should properly have proceeded from Senator Douglas, but it having become apparent that he did not intend to meet Mr. Lincoln, it was thought proper by Mr. Lincoln's friends that the challenge should come from our side. The delay was a matter of courtesy toward Mr. Douglas, and not for the reasons the Senator intimates in his reply. In courteous demeanor, as well as in the honorable conduct of an argument before the people Mr. Douglas will ever find, as in many campaigns he has heretofore found, Mr. Lincoln to be at least his equal.

We much regret that the two candidates cannot canvass the whole State, by speaking together at every county, and in every town of any size or importance. We desire the people to have a fair hearing and a full understanding of the positions, sentiments and argumentative ability of the two men. But the seven meetings proposed, will be better than none. They will give the people of the several Congressional districts an opportunity to get together on the days appointed, in great mass meetings, to hear the great political topics of the day discussed, (fairly and ably we trust) and to "reason together" in the spirit of candor, and with the desire to get at the truth.Let Congressional Mass Meetings be the order of the day.

From the Chicago Times

LINCOLN'S CHALLENGE DOUGLAS' REPLY

On the 9th of July Judge Douglas made his speech in Chicago, and the next evening Mr. Lincoln replied to it. Both gentlemen remained in Chicago for several days thereafter. Subsequently, Judge Douglas proceeded to Springfield to be present at a meeting of the democratic state committeeheld for the purpose of making appointments for public meetings from that period until the election. On his way to Springfield he stopped at Bloomington, Atlanta and Lincoln, and at all these places met Mr. Lincoln and conversed with him. When Mr. Douglas reached Springfield, there were hand-bills conspicuously posted all over the city announcing that Mr. Lincoln would speak that evening. Judge Douglas remained at Springfield two or three days, and then returned to this city. In the meantime the state committee had made out their programme for democratic meetings all over the state, commencing at Clinton, July 27, and ending, we believe, at Atlanta, on the last of October. On Saturday evening last, July 24, Mr. Lincoln, having read in the papers the announcement of Judge Douglas' appointments for August, came up to Chicago, and sent him a note proposing a joint discussion, which note, as well as the reply, we publish below.

Mr. Lincoln evidently has been consulting his own fears and the result likely to follow a separate canvass. He dreaded personally the consequence of a joint discussion, yet he knew that his only chance to obtain respectable audiences, was to make an arrangement to speak at the same meetings with Douglas; between the two causes of dread he has been shivering for nearly a month, and at last, believing that Douglas, having announced his meetings would not change his programme, has allowed his friends to persuade him to make a challenge for a joint discussion. The reply of Judge Douglas, while it explains fully the reasons why he cannot now agree to a joint discussion at all his meetings, tenders Mr. Lincoln a meeting at seven different points in the state. The points designated are important ones; one in each congressional district, and while it disturbs the arrangements heretofore made by the democracy, and communicated to all parts of the state, the proposition of Judge Douglas, if accepted by Mr. Lincoln, will in all probability afford the latter about as much of a joint debate as he will fancy. We doubt very much even if Mr. Lincoln's friends can screw his courage up sufficiently to enable him to accept this offer, whether he will even go through with the seven appointments. We think one, or at all events two of such meetings, will be sufficient to gratify Mr. Lincoln's ambition.

We will see, however, whether he will accept Douglas' offer.

LINCOLN AND DOUGLAS

In today's paper we copy from the Chicago Times a correspondence between Messrs. Lincoln and Douglas, in which the former suggests an arrangement by which the two senatorial candidates will canvass the state together. After Mr. Douglas had issued notice of his appointments to meet the people, prior to which Mr. Lincoln had ample time and opportunity to make and receive a response to such a proposition, it will surprise the public that he has made such an offer. Upon this the Times pointedly comments, and to which Mr. Douglas refers in his reply. He however, offers Mr. Lincoln ample opportunity to discuss the issues between them before the people. Mr. Douglas proposes to meet Mr. Lincoln at one point in each of the congressional districts of the state, except in this and in the 2d district, where they have already spoken. Mr. Lincoln cannot expect his opponent to break his appointments already made, preparations for which the people at the several points are already making; but we have no doubt in the seven encounters proposed by Mr. Douglas, if Mr. Lincoln will accept, he will get enough of debate and discomfiture to last him the balance of his life. Will he accept?

LINCOLN CHALLENGES DOUGLAS TO STUMP
THE STATE WITH HIM

After waiting several weeks hoping that Judge Douglas would, according to the western custom, challenge him to stump the state, Honorable Abram Lincoln sent a note to Judge D. the other day inviting him to make an arrangement to divide time and address the same audiences. The Judge has returned a lengthy reply, excusing himself from accepting such a challenge. His excuse is that he has placed his time at the disposal of the Democratic State Committee, who have made appointments for him which will consume his time until about the middle of October. The excuse will hardly relieve Mr. Douglas from the suspicion that he fears to meet so powerful opponent as Mr. Lincoln in argument before the people. He intimates, in his note, that it was well known that his recent journey to Springfield was made for the purpose of consulting with the state committee, and that if Mr. Lincoln desired to canvass the state with him he should have made the fact known before that consultation was had. How the fact should be well known that Judge Douglas' journey to Springfield was for the purpose of such a consultation as he describes, or any other kind of consultation, is certainly beyond our comprehension. It was not made public through the press and we are not aware that it was announced outside of his immediate circle of friends, if indeed it was announced there. It may be relied upon, at all events, that if Mr. Lincoln had known that his opponent was about to make engagements that would preclude the possibility of arranging a canvass of the state with him, a challenge would have been forthcoming immediately. It was properly Mr. Douglas' duty to challenge Mr. Lincoln, without waiting to receive one.

Mr. Douglas announces, towards the close of his reply, that it is probable that he can meet Mr. Lincoln before the people once in each Congressional district. We hope he will be able to; and in the meantime, if he is disposed to be an honest man, let him desist from such gross misrepresentations of Mr. Lincoln's position as he has thus far indulged in.

AT FREEPORT

Mr. Lincoln having challenged Senator Douglas to meet him on the stump all over the state, the latter declines the general invitation, but agrees to meet him at seven places, as follows: Freeport, Ottawa, Galesburg, Quincy, Alton, Jonesboro, and Charleston, provided Lincoln will come at the times that Douglas' friends may have chosen, if any. Though this is a half way evasion of the challenge, we are glad that we, in Freeport at least, will have an opportunity to hear these two champions from the same stand. We bespeak for them the largest gathering ever known here, and are willing to let the people judge for themselves as to who shall be their choice, after a fair hearing of them both in person.

LINCOLN'S CHALLENGE

The republican organs make a most clumsy effort to have it appear that Senator Douglas declines a general canvass with Mr. Lincoln, because the former dreads the combat! The very tone of these organs, in their silly assertions on this point, denies their sincerity. The idea that a man who has crossed blades in the senate with the strongest intellects of the country, who has as the champion of democratic principles in the senatorial arena, routed all opposition that such a man dreads encounter with Mr. A. Lincoln is an absurdity that can be uttered by his organs only with a ghastly phiz. Mr. Lincoln, if he desired what his organs claim, had ample opportunity to make his proposition. He could have made such an arrangement as would have, had he held out, shown him in withering contrast in every county seat in the state. He was not anxious for the fray! or he would have made his proposition at Chicago, or here, where he had ample opportunity; but he waits until Mr. Douglas makes other arrangements, and advertises them, in a manner that they must, with propriety, be fulfilled, when he banters for battle, knowing his proposition cannot be accepted.

Mr. Douglas' reply to his note affords him fray enough. He has opportunity, at seven different points in the state, to show his metal. If he was good for fifty or a hundred encounters, he certainly ought to be for seven. Will he accept? The joint efforts of the two parties certainly will insure large turn-outs of the people, and we have no doubt the railroads, which have latterly become a nightmare to the republican candidate, will assist, and make, in a "business" way, a "good thing" of it.

Let us have a grand turn-out of the people at one point in each congressional district. The democracy of Illinois will submit the whole case to such popular jurors, called together by the joint effort of the two parties.

DOUGLAS AND LINCOLN

So perverse in their nature are some black republican editors that it seems an impossibility for them to tell the truth. Our home contemporary is of this class. Mark what he says in the following lines:

Lincoln has challenged Douglas to canvass Illinois together, addressing the people from the same stump. Judges Douglas dodges.

Judge Douglas dodges, eh? Well, let us see if he dodges. Here is the correspondence entire between Lincoln and Douglas relating to the matter. No sir, Douglas will meet Lincoln if Lincoln dare to meet Douglas; and the only dodging there will be on the part of the "Little Giant" will take place when the people of Illinois, through their representatives elect, dodge him into the Senatorship again, as they most assuredly will.

DOUGLAS AND LINCOLN ON THE STUMP

We copy below, from the Chicago Times, a correspondence that recently took place between Judge Douglas and Mr. Lincoln, in regard to the plan of the present campaign. Lincoln, having thus far failed to attract a respectable audience, seems to be entirely willing to avail himself of Judge Douglas' great fame and popularity to get up crowds for him to speak to. Nobody seems to care about hearing anything from Lincolnbut the masses of all parties, wherever he goes, turn out to see and hear Douglas. Hence, Lincoln asks him if he won't let him follow along after him and permit him to speak to the crowds that turn out, not to hear him, but to hear Douglas.

In response to the suggestion of Douglas for seven meetings, Lincoln framed a reply. Before it was delivered, he met Douglas by accident near Monticello in the course of the campaign and tendered him the paper. Douglas' reporters took advantage of the incident to ridicule Lincoln.

THE CAMPAIGN

Monticello, July 29, 1858

.... The meeting then adjourned, and Senator Douglas, who was to fill an appointment at Paris on Saturday next, was escorted to the railway station at Bement by the delegation from Okaw, Bement and that vicinity. About two miles out of the town the procession met Mr. Lincoln, who was on his way to Monticello. As he passed, Senator Douglas called to him to stop, that he wanted to see him. Lincoln jumped out of his carriage and shook hands with the Senator, who said to him, "Come, Lincoln, return to Bement. You see we have only a mile or two of people here. I will promise you a much larger meeting there than you will have at Monticello". "No, Judge," replied Lincoln, "I can't. The fact is I did not come over here to make a speech. I don't intend to follow you any more; I don't call this following you. I have come down here from Springfield to see you and give you my reply to your letter. I have it in

my pocket, but I have not compared it with the copy yet. We can compare the two now, can't we?" Senator Douglas told him that he had better compare the two at Monticello, and, when he had his answer ready, send it to him at Bement, where he intended to remain until the one o'clock p. m. train for the East. This Lincoln promised to do, and after again assuring the Senator that he must not consider his visit to Monticello "following" himthat such a "conclusion" would be erroneousthe two separated, after shaking hands....

THE CAMPAIGN IN ILLINOIS

Monticello, Piatt Co, Ills., July 30

When he had finished he was escorted to the railroad depot by a large procession. Col. W. N. Coler, the Democratic nominee for the Legislature in this district, was present during the speech. At its conclusion he was announced to reply to Mr. Lincoln on Friday.

On the way to the railway track the procession of the Judge was met by Abe, who in a kind of nervous-excited manner tumbled out of his carriage, his legs appearing sadly in the way or out of place. Lincoln is looking quite worn out, his face looks even more haggard than when he said it was lean, lank and gaunt. He got to the Judge's carriage with a kind of hop, skip and jump, and then, with a considerable of bowing and scraping, he notified Mr. Douglas that he had an answer to his letter, of which we have spoken heretofore; that it was long, that he had not compared the original and the copy, and could the Judge just wait, that the comparsion might be made by the roadside. Just think of staying out in the middle of a vast prairie, surrounded by hundreds of followers, to compare notes. Douglas of course declined, requesting Mr. L. to compare to his own satisfaction, and then forward the communication.

Lincoln proceeded on his way to Monticello, some of us bearing him company, the Judge returning on his proper route. A meeting was at once organized to hear him speak. He mounted in the Court House Square and thus spoke for about half an hour. He would not speak then, he would, however, read the correspondence with the

Judge, together with the reply he was going to send the Judge, all of which he did.

B. B.

Monticello, July 29

I returned to Monticello to hear Lincoln. He spoke in the grove where Senator Douglas had spoken an hour or two before and promised the people that before the canvass was over he would visit them again in company with Judge Trumbull, who would reply to Douglas. It was expected that he would remain here for a day or two, or follow Senator Douglas to Paris, but he left suddenly on the midnight train for Springfield and one of his friends told me that he did not intend to follow Judge Douglas any more, but was going immediately to Chicago to consult with Cook, Bross, and other friends, and make out a list of his own appointments.
Piatt

Lincoln's reply to the suggestion of Douglas was as follows:
Springfield, July 29, 1858

Hon S. A. Douglas.
Dear Sir: Yours of the 24th in relation to an arrangement to divide time, and address the same audiences, is received; and, in apology for not sooner replying, allow me to say, that when I sat by you at dinner yesterday, I was not aware that you had answered my note, nor, certainly that my own note had been presented to you. An hour after, I saw a copy of your answer in the Chicago Times, and reaching home, I found the original awaiting me. Protesting that your insinuations of attempted unfairness on my part are unjust, and with the hope that you did not very considerately make them, I proceed to reply. To your statement that "It has been suggested, recently, that an arrangement had been made to bring out a third candidate for the United States Senate, who, with yourself, should canvass the State in opposition to me," etc., I can only say, that such suggestion must have been made by yourself, for certainly none such has been made by or to me, or otherwise, to my knowledge. Surely you did not deliberately conclude, as you insinuate, that I was expecting to draw you into an arrangement of terms, to be agreed on by yourself, by which a third candidate and myself, "in concert, might be able to take the opening and closing speech in every case."
As to your surprise that I did not sooner make the proposal to divide time with you, I can only say, I made it as soon as I resolved to make it. I did not know but that such proposal would come from you; I waited, respectfully to see. It may have been well known to you that you went to Springfield for the purpose of agreeing on the plan of campaign; but it was not so known to me. When your appointments were announced in the papers, extending

only to the 21st of August, I, for the first time considered it certain that you would make no proposal to me, and then resolved that, if my friends concurred, I would make one to you. As soon thereafter as I could see and consult with friends satisfactorily, I did make the proposal. It did not occur to me that the proposed arrangement could derange your plans after the latest of your appointments already made. After that, there was, before the election, largely over two months of clear time.

For you to say that we have already spoken at Chicago and Springfield, and that on both occasions I had the concluding speech, is hardly a fair statement. The truth rather is this: At Chicago, July 9th, you made a carefully prepared conclusion on my speech of June 16th. Twenty-four hours after, I made a hasty conclusion on yours of the 9th. You had six days to prepare, and concluded on me again at Bloomington on the 16th. Twenty-four hours after, I concluded again on you at Springfield. In the mean time, you had made another conclusion on me at Springfield, which I did not hear, and of the contents of which I knew nothing when I spoke; so that your speech made in daylight, and mine at night, of the 17th, at Springfield, were both made in perfect independence of each other. The dates of making all these speeches will show, I think, that in the matter of time for preparation, the advantage has all been on your side, and that none of the external circumstances have stood to my advantage.

I agree to an arrangement for us to speak at the seven places you have named, and at your own times, provided you name the times at once, so that I, as well as you, can have to myself the time not covered by the arrangement. As to the other details, I wish perfect reciprocity and no more. I wish as much time as you, and that conclusions shall alternate. That is all.

Your obedient servant,

A. Lincoln

P. S. As matters now stand, I shall be at no more of your exclusive meetings; and for about a week from today a letter from you will reach me at Springfield.

A. L.

To this Mr. Douglas replied:

Bement, Piatt Co., Ill., July 30, 1858

Dear Sir: Your letter dated yesterday, accepting my proposition for a joint discussion at one prominent point in each Congressional District, as stated in my previous letter, was received this morning.

The times and places designated are as follows:

Ottawa, LaSalle County, August 21, 1858

Freeport., Stephenson County, " 27,"
Jonesboro, Union County, September 15,"
Charleston, Coles County, " 18,"
Galesburg, Knox County, October 7,"
Quincy, Adams County, " 13,"
Alton, Madison County, " 15,"
I agree to your suggestion that we shall alternately open and close the discussion. I will speak at Ottawa one hour, you can reply, occupying an hour and a half, and I will then follow for half an hour. At Freeport, you shall open the discussion and speak one hour; I will follow for an hour and a half, and you can then reply for half an hour. We will alternate in like manner in each successive place.
Very respectfully, your obedient servant,
S. A. Douglas

Hon. A. Lincoln, Springfield, Ill.

This arrangement was accepted by Mr. Lincoln:

Springfield, July 31, 1858

Hon. S. A. Douglas.
Dear Sir: Yours of yesterday, naming places, times, and terms, for joint discussions between us, was received this morning. Although, by the terms, as you propose, you take four openings and closes, to my three, I accede, and thus close the arrangement. I direct this to you at Hillsboro, and shall try to have both your letter and this appear in the Journal and Register of Monday morning.
A. Lincoln
Your obedient servant,
THE AGREEMENT BETWEEN SENATOR DOUGLAS AND MR. LINCOLN.

We received yesterday, and print this morning, the final correspondence between Senator Douglas and Mr. Lincoln, in relation to CONGRESSIONAL MAP OF ILLINOIS, 1858 Showing places where the seven debates were held, numbered in order addressing the people in company. Those readers who examine the letter of our Monticello correspondent will learn somewhat of the circumstances which attended the conclusion of this arrangement. Mr. Lincoln's letter is dated Springfield, but it was sent by the author from some place in Piatt county to Senator Douglas in Bement. We are not disposed to criticise too harshly the style of Mr. Lincoln's letter. It is now printed and speaks for itself its own praise or condemnation. But, the public will have their opinion of it, and it can be none other than that it is as badly conceived as bunglingly expressed. We hope, however, that we have seen the "conclusion" of the correspondence, and do not question that by the time Mr. Lincoln has "concluded" on Senator Douglas, once or twice, and permitted Senator Douglas to "conclude" on him an equal number of times, he will "conclude" that he better haul off and lay by for repairs.

We need not describe the arrangement, as it is made fully to appear in the correspondence itself.

MR. LINCOLN'S CHALLENGE TO MR. DOUGLAS
REJOINDER OF MR. LINCOLN

We have already published the letter of Mr. Lincoln challenging Mr. Douglas to a joint canvass of the State, and also the letter of Mr. Douglas in reply, declining the invitation in the most pettifogging and cowardly manner. Today we publish a rejoinder of Mr. Lincoln, exposing the flimsy pretexts upon which Mr. Douglas places his declension and at the same time cordially responding to that part of the reply in which Mr. Douglas reluctantly consents to allow himself to be used up by Mr. Lincoln at seven different places. It is clear that Mr. Douglas is not fond of Mr. Lincoln's rough handling and is anxious to get out of an ugly scrape on any terms. In this matter Douglas goes on the principle that discretion is the better part of valor.

We knew from the first that Douglas would not dare to make a general canvass of the state with Lincoln. He had to run away from that gentleman in 1854 and dared not stand his broadsides now. If he dared not meet Lincoln in the first dawnings of his conspiracy to Africanize the whole American Continent, of course he would object still more to such a canvass in 1858, when the evidences of that conspiracy are so numerous and overwhelming that even his audacity shrinks from denying it. But we did expect that Mr. Douglas would

at least put his refusal on some more plausible ground than a mere squibble. The idea that Mr. Douglas is unable to meet Mr. Lincoln in debate because forsooth a Democratic Central Committee had already made some half dozen appointments for him, is pitifuljust as though those appointments could not be changed, or so modified as also to embrace a discussion with

Mr. Lincoln or leaving those appointments out of the question, just as though there was not yet remaining full two months in which to make the canvass with Mr. Lincoln! However it is viewed, Mr. Douglas' attempt to Skulk behind a Central Committee, is a cowardly showing of the white feather.

The Times finds fault with Mr. Lincoln's letter to Mr. Douglas because it is "bunglingly expressed."

Our neighbor should recollect that he has not the advantage of having the Douglas candidate for Superintendent of Public Instruction to correct it for him!

DISCUSSION BETWEEN MESSRS. DOUGLAS AND LINCOLN

We were furnished on Saturday, by Mr. Lincoln, with the following correspondence, from which it will be seen that he agrees to meet Mr. Douglas in discussion at seven points in the state, which are named in the note of the letter. Mr. Lincoln cannot forego, even in this brief note, the expression of the idea uppermost with him, that he is "a victim," Douglas has one more "opening" than himself, which, if it were not so, Mr. Lincoln would have one more than Mr. Douglas. As we are told by Mr. Lincoln's organs that Douglas felt incapable of debating successfully with Mr. L., the latter should have forborne his lament, in a spirit of magnanimity.

Now there is a bit of egotism in all this, pardonable, probably, in view of Mr. Lincoln's extremity. Why had he, any more than Wentworth, or Browning, or Gillespie, or Palmer, or Dougherty, or Judd, or any other republican or Danite notability, a right to expect a challenge for debate from Douglas. True, Lincoln had thrust himself before all the reception meetings gotten up in honor of Mr. Douglas, and had taken shape as a senatorial candidate; but as Mr. Douglas suggests, there are others with similar aspirations. He had in this manner of doubtful propriety, made himself a figure out of place, but we cannot see that the circumstances were such as to induce Mr. Douglas to single him out from the number of his opponentsblack republican and Danite, and challenge him to a general canvass. Mr. Lincoln's political necessities may have needed this boosting of him into prominence, but he is scarcely justified in lamenting that Mr. Douglas did not contribute to it.

Mr. Douglas, as a representative of his state in the senate, was a prominent actor in the exciting debates of the last session. His action and his motives therefor had been condemned and impugned, and he had concluded, on his return home, to go before his constituents to render an account of the course he had deemed proper to pursue, as well as to advocate the principles, policy and the election of the candidates of his party. Mr. Lincoln was as well qualified to know that Mr. Douglas came to this city to arrange with his party friends for this purpose, as was Mr. Douglas that Mr. Lincoln's party friends had arranged that he was to champion their cause; and as such, if it was his desire to have had a general canvass, single-handed, he could have made it known at the thresholdat Chicago. Why he did not do it, is simply because he had not "resolved" to do it and we think he did not resolve to do it because he thought he could cut a better figure by waiting until Mr. Douglas had made other arrangements, and then pompously send a challenge which he knew could not be accepted.

Mr. Lincoln knew it was Mr. Douglas' intention to canvass the state long before Mr. D's return home. If it was his desire to canvass with himif it was the desire of his party that he should do so, he should have met the "lion," with a watchful resistance, at the gate, and not have waited for his terms, and the mode and manner of being eaten up.

This bit of pettifogging jugglery on the part of Mr. Lincoln and his backers can only be viewed as such by the people of the state. The twaddle of his organ about Douglas' dread of his prowess is unworthy of comment. Mr. Douglas' agreement to meet him as proposed in the correspondence above, which could not, under the circumstances, be declined by Mr. Lincoln, is, doubtless, more than they bargained for in their epistolary efforts to make a brave front on paper, as they will certainly learn before they are through with a small portion of the large job they profess to bid for.

CHAPTER IV. REPORTING THE DEBATES

MR. HORACE WHITE

Mr. White, the official reporter of the Debates for the Chicago Press and Tribune, was born in New Hampshire in 1834. When three years of age, he was taken with the family to Wisconsin Territory, where the city of Beloit now stands. In 1849, Horace entered Beloit College, was graduated in 1853, and became a reporter on the Chicago Evening Journal. In 1857 he spent a short time in Kansas, returning to Chicago to become an editorial writer on the Chicago Press and Tribune. While holding this position, he was designated as chief correspondent to accompany Abraham Lincoln in 1858 on his campaign against Stephen A. Douglas for the United States senatorship.

The notable features of this campaign were given to the public chiefly through Mr. White's letters to the Chicago Tribune, and were subsequently condensed by him at the instance of William H. Herndon and published in the latter's Life of Lincoln (2d ed., D. Appleton and Co., New York). In 1861 Mr. White was sent to Washington as correspondent of the Chicago Tribune, and while there he filled successfully the places of clerk of the Senate Committee on Military Affairs and clerk in the War Department. In the latter capacity he was assigned to the special service of P. H. Watson, assistant secretary of war, and later of Edwin M. Stanton, secretary. In 1865 he became part owner and chief editor of the Chicago Tribune, which place he filled until September, 1874, when he resigned and was succeeded by Joseph Medill; he spent the year 1875 in Europe. In 1877 he removed to New York and became associated with Henry Villard in the latter 's railroad enterprises, especially that of the Oregon Railway and Navigation Co., of which he was treasurer for the next few years. In 1881 he joined with Mr. Villard in the purchase of the New York Evening Post, of which he became the president and one of the editors, in conjunction with Carl Schurz and

Edwin L. Godkin. Mr. Schurz retired in 1884, Mr. Godkin in 1899, and Mr. White in 1903. Mr. White is best known by his contributions to the various campaigns for sound money that have been fought in the political arena since the close of the Civil War. In addition to his editorial work he has been a frequent contributor to the magazines and pamphlet literature of that period. He resides (1908) in New York City.

It was my good fortune to accompany Mr. Lincoln during his political campaign against Senator Douglas in 1858, not only at the joint debates but also at most of the smaller meetings where his competitor was not present. We traveled together many thousands of miles. I was in the employ of the Chicago Tribune, then called the Press and Tribune. Senator Douglas had entered upon his campaign with two short-hand reporters, James B. Sheridan and Henry Binmore, whose duty it was to "write it up" in the columns of the Chicago Times. The necessity of counteracting or matching that force became apparent very soon, and I was chosen to write up Mr. Lincoln's campaign.

I was not a short-hand reporter. The verbatim reporting for the Chicago Tribune in the joint debates was done by Mr. Robert R. Hitt, late assistant secretary of state..... Verbatim reporting was a new feature in journalism in Chicago and Mr, Hitt was the pioneer thereof. The publication of Senator Douglas' opening speech in that campaign, delivered on the evening of July 9, by the Tribune the next morning, was a feat hitherto unexampled in the West, and most mortifying to the Democratic newspaper, the Times, and to Sheridan and Binmore,

HORACE WHITE

All of the seven joint debates were reported by Mr. Hitt for the Tribune, the manuscript passing through my hands before going to the printers, but no changes were made by me except in a few cases where confusion on the platform, or the blowing of the wind, had caused some slight hiatus or evident mistake in catching the speaker's words. I could not resist the temptation to italicise a few passages in Mr. Lincoln 's speeches, where his manner of delivery had been especially emphatic.

Here I was joined by Mr. Hitt and also by Mr. Chester P. Dewey of the New York Evening Post, who remained with us until the end of the campaign. Hither, also, came quite an army of young newspaper men, among whom was Henry Villard, in behalf of Forney's Philadelphia Press.

MR. ROBERT R. HITT

Robert Roberts Hitt was born in Urbana, Champaign County, Ohio, January 16, 1834. In 1837, the Hitts moved to Illinois and with their following settled in Ogle County, and established what became the village of Mount Morris. Educated at the Rock River Seminary at Mount Morris, an institution founded by his father and uncle, and later graduated from the Asbury (now Depauw) University of Indiana, the subject of this sketch trained himself in the art of phonography and in 1856 opened an office in Chicago and established himself as a court and newspaper shorthand reporter, the first expert stenographer permanently located in that city. His work as a stenographer first brought him into the notice of Abraham Lincoln, then practicing law, and later as a newspaper reporter in reporting the campaign speeches of Lincoln and other prominent orators of the day, including Douglas, Logan, Lovejoy, and indeed of all the great speakers of the Middle West of that time. During the Lincoln-Doug- las debates he was the verbatim reporter, receiving the highest praise from Mr. Lincoln for the accuracy of his work.

During the sessions of 1858, 1859, and 1860, Mr. Hitt was the official stenographer of the Illinois legislature, having the contract for both the senate and the house. In 1867 and 1868 he made a tour of Europe and Asia, daily taking down in shorthand notes his impressions of the peoples and conditions of the countries and places visited. Upon his return he was again employed by the government in confidential cases, including missions to Santo Domingo and to the southern states to investigate the Ku Klux Klan, after which he became private secretary to Senator O. P. Morton, and in December of the same year was appointed secretary of legation at Paris, by President Grant, which position he held for six years.

In 1880, upon the request of Mr. Blaine, then secretary of state, President

Garfield appointed him assistant secretary, which position he resigned to become a candidate for Congress, to which he was elected in 1882. He served continuously from the Forty-eighth to the Fifty-eighth Congress. While serving his twelfth term, Mr. Hitt died on September 20, 1906 at Narragansett Pier, Rhode Island.

AN INTERVIEW WITH HON. R. R. HITT

When I was a lad of nearly fifteen, I saw some little pamphlets which were handed me by a man named Pickard, in 1850, in advocacy of phonetic reform, and it was through the advertisements in them that I procured the phonographic manuals. From these works I obtained enough knowledge of the principles and rules of shorthand to begin to use it.

The first fruitful use of it was in taking notes of lectures at college. After graduating at Mt. Morris College I went to New Orleans, constantly practicing the art and gaining speed. In the spring of 1857 I returned to Illinois, then removed to Chicago and began to report

ROBERT R. HITT

From a daguerreotype made in 1858, and loaned by Mrs. Hitt, of Washington, D C
court cases. In 1858 the contest between Stephen A. Douglas and Mr. Lincoln for the Senate brought Mr. Lincoln into national view. Seven debates were arranged between them and I was employed to report them on the Republican side.

There was no one to assist in reporting but a young man named Laraminie from Montreal, who was a skillful reader of shorthand and could transcribe my notes with perfect accuracy. At Quincy, Illinois, where one of the debates was held, he took the train for Chicago, which left before the debate was finished, carrying with him my notes of the earlier part of the debate, and I first saw the work printed in a newspaper. Mr. Lincoln never saw the report of any of the debates. I mention this as it was often charged at that time in the fury of partisan warfare that Mr. Lincoln's speeches were doctored and almost re-written before they were printed; that this was necessary because he was so petty a creature in ability, in thought, in style, in speaking when compared with the matchless Douglas.

To tell the story of Mr. Hitt's public career with anything like completeness would require columns of space. He first came into the public eye just after he left college. He had learned the system of shorthand then in use and was probably the only stenographer in the West at that time who could take a speech verbatim as it was delivered from the rostrum.

Abraham Lincoln had heard of his rare accomplishment and made a requisition on the young man to report the Lincoln-Douglas debate at Freeport, Illinois. It is chronicled that when the debate was about to begin, Mr. Lincoln lifted his long form from a chair, looked out over the immense audience, and shouted, "Where's Hitt? Is Hitt present?"

The future representative and possible vice-president was far out on the edge of the crowd.

"Here I am, Mr. Lincoln," he cried, "but I can't get through this crowd to the stand". Whereupon strong men lifted the frail, slender young man into the air and passed him along over the heads of the crowd to the platform. Mr. Hitt took complete notes of the speech and afterward transcribed most of them himself. Some of Mr. Lincoln's political enemies, who had brought an indictment of illiteracy against the gaunt Illinois statesman, charged Mr. Hitt with "doctoring" the English of the speech, but he denied that he had taken any liberties with Lincoln's phraseology..... His notes of the Lincoln-Douglas debates would be invaluable literary documents today, but he did not preserve them.... Because of the prestige growing out of his services in the Lincoln-Douglas debate, he was selected to make the official report of the trouble that arose in 1860 in the Department of Missouri under General Fremont.

HENRY BINMORE

Henty Binmore was born in London, England, September 23, 1833; educated in the schools of England and at Wickhall College, and came to Montreal, Canada, at the age of 16. He at once entered the profession of journalism and invented a system of phonographic reporting peculiar to himself. With it he was able to attain a desirable speed, but could not exchange reading with other systems. He continued at newspaper work in Montreal, New York, and St. Louis for several years, including a term as reporter in the Missouri state senate. In 1858 he was employed on the St. Louis Republican, a Douglas organ, and was sent to Illinois to report the triumphant home-coming of the senator. His reports appearing in the Republican showed such skill in his art that he was employed by the Chicago Times, the official newspaper of Douglas, to report the set debates with Lincoln. He shared this task with James B. Sheridan, a regular phonographic reporter, brought from Philadelphia.

At the close of the campaign, Mr. Binmore became a private secretary to Douglas and in 1860 was made reporter in the House of Representatives. From this position he resigned to accept a secretarial appointment on the staff of General Prentiss and later on that of General Hurlbut. At the close of the war, he returned to Chicago, became a law reporter, was admitted to the bar, and died in that city, November 4, 1907. He left an unpublished manuscript on the art and experiences of reportorial writing.

From a contemporary photograph in the possession of the family, Chicago

JAMES B. SHERIDAN

The art of phonography was early developed in Philadelphia where was located a prominent school. Among its early disciples was Mr. Sheridan, who became a prominent reporter on Forney's Philadelphia Press. Forney espoused the cause of Douglas in his breach with Buchanan and when the senator entered upon his great canvass for re-election, Forney sent Sheridan to Illinois to follow the campaign. It was not the original intention to have him remain throughout the autumn, but the value of his services as a reporter was so evident that he was employed to take the debates for the Democratic Chicago Times, in connection with Mr. Binmore. He continued to write descriptive articles for the Press, many of the quotations from that paper printed in this volume being no doubt contributed by him.

At the close of the campaign, Sheridan went to New York, enlisted as a northern Democrat in the Civil War, attained the rank of colonel, and later became the official reporter of the New York Supreme Court. In 1875, he was elected justice of the Marine Court of New York City. He died about 1905.

Owing to the prevalent partisan feeling, there was complaint on both sides of unfairness in reporting the debates. Immediately after the appearance in print of the speeches in the first debate, each side accused the other of misrepresenting the ideas expressed by its spokesman. The Republican press claimed that Lincoln was not given a fair report, and the Democratic editors replied that Lincoln was by nature ungrammatical and uncouth in his utterances. It is true that the variations to be noted in Mr. Lincoln's speeches as reported in the Republican and in the Democratic papers decreased steadily throughout the campaign. Quite naturally the Democratic reporters did not exercise the same care in taking the utterances of Mr. Lincoln as with those of Mr. Douglas, and vice versa. Mr. White described later the difficulties under which the reporting was donethe open air, the rude platforms, the lack of accommodations for writing, the jostling of the crowds of people, and the occasional puffs of wind which played havoc with sheets of paper.

LINCOLN'S SPEECH

We delayed the issue of our Sunday morning's paper some hours in order that we might publish in full the speeches of Lincoln and Douglas, at Ottawa. We had two phonographic reporters there to report these speeches. One of them (Mr. Sheridan) we have known personally for years, and know him to be one of the most accomplished phonographers in the United States Senate. The other (Mr. Binmore) is reputed to be a most excellent reporter, and having had occasion to mark the manner in which he has on several occasions executed his duty, we are satisfied that he is not only a competent but a most faithful reporter. These two gentlemen reported the two speeches, and they, shortly after their arrival in Chicago from Ottawa, commenced transcribing the speeches from their notes. We publish both speeches as they were furnished us by the reporters.

THE SPEECHES AT OTTAWA

Any person who heard at Ottawa the speech of Abraham, alias Old Abe, alias Abe, alias "Spot," Lincoln, must have been astonished at the report of that speech as it appeared in the Press and Tribune of this city. Our version of it was literal. No man, who heard it delivered, could fail to recognize and acknowledge the fidelity of our reporters. We did not attempt, much, to "fix up" the bungling effort; that was not our business. Lincoln should have learned, before this, to "rake after" himselfor rather to supersede the necessity of "raking after" by taking heed to his own thoughts and expressions. If he ever gets into the United States Senateof which

JAMES B. SHERIDAN

From a photograph in the possession of Mrs. Sheridan, New York, made about 1857

there is no earthly probabilityhe will have to do that; in the congressional arena, the words of debaters are snatched from their lips, as it were, and immediately enter into and become a permanent part of the literature of the country. But it seems, from the difference between the two versions of Lincoln's speech, that the Republicans have a candidate for the Senate of whose bad rhetoric and horrible jargon they are ashamed, upon which before they would publish it, they called a council of "literary" men, to discuss, re-construct and re-write; they dare not allow Lincoln to go into print in his own dress; and abuse us, the Times, for reporting him literally.

We also printed Senator Douglas literally. Our accomplished reporters alone are responsible to us for the accuracy of our version of both speeches. There is no orator in America more correct in rhetoric, more clear in ideas, more direct in purpose, in all his public addresses, than Stephen A. Douglas. That this is so, is not our fault, but rather it is the pride of the Democracy of Illinois and of the Union.

OUTRAGEOUS FRAUDS

One Hundred and Eighty Mutilations Made in Lincoln's Speech by The Chicago Times! !

We had heard of the numerous frauds to which the Douglas party resort to mislead the public mind, beginning with the forgery of the platform at Ottawa and ending with Douglas' declaration that Mr. Lincoln is hired by the Illinois Central Railroad Company, at $5,000 per year, to cheat the State of its 7 per cent, dividends of the earnings of the Road (the very post occupied by Mr. Douglas), but were not prepared for such rascality as is exhibited in the Times' report of the debate in this place. There is scarcely a correctly reported paragraph in the whole speech! Many sentences are dropped out which were absolutely necessary for the sense; many are transposed so as to read wrong end first; many are made to read exactly the opposite of the orator's intention, and the whole aim has been to blunt the keen edge of Mr. Lincoln's wit, to mar the beauty of his most eloquent passages, and make him talk like a booby, a half-witted numbskull. By placing him thus before their readers they hope to disgust the people with Mr. Lincoln, and at least keep them at home if they do not vote for Douglas. Even that beautiful apostrophe, quoted from the "Revered Clay," as Douglas hypocritically called him at the Bancroft House, could not go unmutilated.

We have taken the pains to go over the reports of the speeches carefully and note the material alterationssaying nothing of long passages, where the Times' Reporter appeared to aim only at the sense, without giving the languageand find that the number One Hundred and Eighty!

We believe that an action for libel would hold against these villians, and they richly deserve the prosecution.

GARBLING SPEECHES THE OLD CHARGE

We do not mean, by this remark, to cast any imputation of unfairness on Mr. Hitt, the reporter for the Press and Tribune; such imputation would be unjust, as we have reason to believe. Our controversy is not with the reporter at all; for even if he should maltreat Senator Douglas' speeches, he would do so under instructions; he being the employee of our neighbor, he could not relieve the editors of the odium of the fact. But such are the facts; we give them, not because we feel very deeply on this point, but to put the public right with regard to them. We can prove their proof by Mr. Hitt himself, if he will go upon the stand under oath. Even, however, after Senator Douglas' speeches are marredby striking out words, here and there, by mangling sentences to hide their meaning, by mis-punctuations, etc. etc.and after re-writing and polishing the speeches of Lincoln, those of Douglas so much excelled those of his opponent, in all respects, that we cannot find it in our hearts to complain much. Poor Lincoln requires some such advantagethough it be meanin his contest with the irresistible advocate of liberal principlesthe acknowledged champion of living principles in Illinois.

Douglas carries around with him a reporter by the name of Sheridan whose business it is to garble the speeches of Mr. Lincoln, and amend and elaborate those of Douglas, for the Times. As almost everybody present on Wednesday could hear Mr. Lincoln distinctly, and not a hundred in the crowd could understand Douglas, we are curious to see the report that this fellow Sheridan will give of the speeches. Our word for it, he will serve his master to the best of his ability, and lie about the whole proceedings.

Made in the USA
Coppell, TX
21 September 2023

21846141R00111